The Tao of Money

How to Order:

Single copies may be ordered from Prima Publishing, P.O. Box 1260BK, Rocklin, CA 95677; telephone (916) 786-0426. Quantity discounts are also available. On your letterhead, include information regarding the intended use of the books and the number of books you wish to purchase.

The Tao of Money

Six Simple Principles
for Achieving Financial Harmony

Ivan Hoffman

Prima Publishing
P.O. Box 1260BK
Rocklin, CA 95677
(916)786-0426

Production by Janis Paris, Bookman Productions
Copyediting by Carol Henry
Indexing by Nancy Freedom
Typography by Bookman Productions
Interior design by Judith Levinson, Bookman Productions
Cover design by Lindy Dunlavey, The Dunlavey Studio,
    Sacramento

Library of Congress Cataloging-in-Publication Data

Hoffman, Ivan.
    The Tao of money : six simple principles for
achieving financial harmony / Ivan Hoffman.
        p. cm.
    Includes index.
    ISBN 1-55958-436-X (pbk.)
    1. Finance, Personal.   2. Financial security.
    3. Taoism-Miscellanea.   I. Title
HG179.H596   1994   93-34370
332.024—dc20   CIP

94 95 96 97 98 RRD 10 9 8 7 6 5 4 3 2 1
Printed in the United States of America

This book is dedicated to Susan, who gave me the courage to change my life; to my children, Garrett and Jordan, who, I hope, see that it is in our power to do so; to Murray, my dog, who, in giving me back more love than I could imagine ever existed, opened me up to myself; to my mother and my late father; and to Rabbi Steven Reuben, who continues to stoke my creative fire.

Contents

Acknowledgments

I wish to gratefully thank Jennifer Basye and Andi Reese Brady at Prima, whose editorial assistance has been invaluable.

Prologue

This book follows my first, *The Tao of Love*, and I might say that it would be helpful to the reader of *The Tao of Money* to go back and read *The Tao of Love*. Further, anyone who has read the first book should definitely continue with this one, because it is the natural sequel. It's all part of my feeling that nothing can change in the "outer world" until we change in our "inner world." To be open to new ideas about the world at large, we must first, it seems to me, be open to new ideas about our own selves. This we can do only if we are self-secure and trusting about our roles in the universe. God, Tao, the universe are all, to my way of thinking, the same as love. Love is, accordingly, the most basic of building tools and so it came first.

I urge you to have an open mind as you turn this book's pages. The Six Simple Principles for Achieving Financial Harmony described herein are not about personal finances. Rather, they refer to global financial harmony, which may arise if we reach a place of personal financial harmony. My approach is to show how, by examining our own views about money, we might be able to effect change and create harmony in the way we look at money universally. My view of money is more expansive than the way it is usually treated. I use the term *money* standing alone, as well as in relation to other issues; for, like all things in the universe, nothing exists by itself, and *money* gets part of its very definition by its role in other issues. *The Tao of Money* attempts to draw the integral connections among issues that might otherwise seem unconnected, better to enable us to seek potential solutions.

Ivan

The Premise

The world is simply not working. It may be working for some, but if it is not working for all, then sooner or later it will stop working for everyone. We have severe worldwide unemployment, job elimination, hunger, homelessness, millions of displaced persons, ecological destruction, war. Whether we personally are victims of any of these symptoms directly, we are all their victims indirectly. The social costs to each of us, costs that ultimately come down to money in one form or another, are enormous.

It is, therefore, my intent to propose some very new ideas about how we might let the world work. And central to these ideas is that our views about money need to be reexamined, for those views, and the real-world policies and programs that follow along from them, are one of the key reasons why the world is not working.

Money is, to a very large degree, a key element in how most of us define ourselves. Whether we have money or lack it, it tells many of us who we think we are and who we believe we are not. By money, I mean not just the cash in our pockets that we take to the video store, but money in the larger sense. I mean the way in which we use money for good or for ill. This book is about money, but it is also about the social impact that money has upon each of our individual lives and on the world as a whole. This book is about how money is integral, not only to obvious social problems, but also to those that seem less direct. This book is about war and peace, for war and peace are, most frequently, about money.

If you do not feel totally secure about your personal economic situations; if you fear money, either not having it or having too much of it; if you wonder, aloud or to yourself, whether the way the world is, is the way it must be; if you believe that your taxes are either too high or are not being used as you would like by the various governments that receive those taxes; if you think that "someone should do something about IT" (whatever IT is); if you feel that the significant changes taking place in the world have left you behind, feeling almost as disposable as a hamburger container —then you should read on.

We are, all of us in our individual ways, the products of the economic changes that affect what seems to be the outside world. I say "seems to be the outside world" because the outside world is really only our individual inside worlds played out on a larger screen. This outer world's changes mirror changes in our individual lives. But it is also true that the changes in our individual lives make up the changes we see in the world as a whole. The world is, after all, nothing more than all of us added up together. And so this book is about how we might change the economic and social conditions that are the result of our own viewpoints about money, by changing the viewpoints themselves.

These points of view have been and will continue to be put to severe tests during the last 20 years leading up to today and into the next century. We must examine how our points of view need to be altered to fit these significantly changed circumstances.

For example, the chaos of Eastern Europe, the rise of the Asian "tigers" of Korea, Taiwan, and Malaysia as monetary superpowers, the economic dominance of Japan, the ebbing of the oil cartel's powers, the social and economic destruction felt by those who have never known unemployment and who embody the so-called American Dream—all find their origins in our own ideas about money. The lack of U.S. competitiveness in world markets today is directly connected to our individual mind-sets about money and its related social issues. The lack of faith we seem to have in our nation's direction stems from our decisions made over the past 50 years to elect leaders who pandered to and were products of our need for fear instead of our need for vision.

Of course, we tend not to think about these "external" events as having anything to do with our own lives, but merely things we read about in the paper or see on the television news, events to *tsk-tsk* our tongues at. We ignore them because they are things that happen to someone else, failing to acknowledge, even to ourselves, that we, too, are living hand-to-mouth and that many of us are but a paycheck or two away from homelessness and economic chaos.

Yet all of everything that goes on in the "outer" world is but a reflection of our personal, internal worlds. The way we think about ourselves in relation to money—as well as to a whole host of other, perhaps more personal, spiritual issues—gets translated into the very problems we see as divorced from us. And, because—like Taoism itself—everything is connected to everything else, those "external" events in turn affect us personally, internally, spiritually. Just ask anyone without a job because a factory has closed due to foreign imports how being unemployed has affected his or her emotional and spiritual life.

The monetary changes going on in this outer world, like the changes in many other social issues, are the result of the forces of balance seeking to break out of centuries of human artifices. Humanity has placed so many restrictions on natural processes, including the natural processes of money, that the great social upheavals we see happening today are really the result of these restrictions breaking apart. The changes taking place are the natural forces of the universe trying to find their own level and struggling against the forces of resistance. These restrictions have included artificial boundaries between nations, tariffs and other restraints on free trade, subsidies favoring one market over another, economic theories such as communism and capitalism that have been elevated to greater importance than helping the very people they were designed to help. We are the cause of the resistance to these changes and are thus also the end product of that resistance. We are both the actors and the audience.

As with all social issues, we have the choice to continue to resist and attempt to restrain things by supporting the economic status quo, or to let go and allow the changes to occur, taking the opportunity to benefit from them. The choices we make in how we will handle economic changes throughout the world depend, to a large degree, on how comfortable we are with our ability to deal with change in our personal lives. In turn, this depends to a large degree on how comfortable we are within the deepest recesses of our souls about who we are. What we may find is that the problems we all claim we seek to change will not change unless we begin to see our connection to those problems and unless we are willing to get down to very fundamental issues.

The Six Simple Principles for Achieving Financial Harmony that form the basis of this book are really about how we can learn to translate our views about who we are and how we look at money into changed policies about money and its related social consequences. In the process, we can reach a place of economic peace, monetary balance, and, ultimately, harmony. The use of the term *simple* is not meant to be facetious, for I suggest that once we get to the place in our growth where we see the connections, the changes can indeed be simple. When they become that clear to us, we slap ourselves on the forehead, wondering how we did not see the answers before.

Until then, I agree that "peace"—for that is what I am speaking about—is a very difficult idea. But once we see how we are the cause of policies, once we find our personal place in the scheme of things, certain principles can become evident in ways we could not previously imagine.

As we then change our internal point of view about money, the world can become a changed place. And as changes in the outer world begin to mirror changes in our personal world, we may find that we begin to become more comfortable with ourselves in relation to money. Ask anyone who has found a job in a new industry after being laid off from an old and dying one.

All the problems we collectively face today have been created by *us* as a result of our own internal points of view. As we each see our private world and how this melds into the collective humanity, our individual visions become enlarged. Our 8mm personal points of view become wide-angle screens with stereo sound. We need to see the larger picture, the *gestalt*, of our situation through a broader lens. But our vision is narrowed by our narrow views, as though we are seeing the world from the bottom of a deep well.

Our ideas are awry because we are in touch with neither ourselves nor with the Earth. Indeed, *because* we are not in touch with ourselves, we are not in touch with the Earth. We do not consider ourselves a part of the Earth but rather apart from it. We have always felt that we are the masters of our fate, the captains of our soul. We have told ourselves that we can dominate and control nature. In truth, everything that we have told ourselves is a lie.

We search for solutions within our "advanced" ideas for the great problems that we face, but all our attempted solutions point outward, at external causes and external solutions. It is never us, it is "Them," whoever *They* may be at any given moment. The disembodied IT is always victimizing us. We have created a duality, a separation of ourselves from ourselves. We have divorced ourselves from our work and our relationship to money as though work and money were only means to an end, the end being different from the means. We have excused ourselves from personal responsibility for our condition.

Given a cursory glance, like a termite-infested old house, the facade that is our home appears whole and sound. We never notice that underneath, below the surface, the entire structure is being eaten away. We ignore the waste droppings and sawdust, until one day, seemingly suddenly but in reality inevitably, our home just collapses. We are the last to know what was going on because we never took the time to get in tune with our home, to hear its creaks, to feel its unsteadiness. If we heard, if we saw, if we felt, we ignored—thinking it would go away. We are similarly in danger of having our economic world collapse around us while we pretend that everything is fine. We spend and consume, ignoring the dangers not only to our own individual security but to the security of the world as a whole. "Really, everything is just fine. Really!" we say, as though the exclamation point will make the point. It's as ridiculous as yelling ever more loudly in English at someone who does not speak our language.

Just as our personal economic conditions may be out of balance—the results of recession, unemployment, and job displacement—so are the economic systems of the world out of balance. The former Soviet system, for example, was an artificial economic and social construct that depended on fear and killing to keep it together. The U.S. economic system depends upon restrictions and protections that benefit some to the detriment of others. The Soviet system has failed. The U.S. system is failing, too, if with less drama. The differences are merely in degree—except, of course, from the vantage point of the people who are being hurt by such failures. To them it does not matter whether they are the victims of the failure of communism or capitalism. Being without food in Russia is not substantially different from being without food in Rochester.

The trends in our collective decline are long-term and not easily seen by those who think a "quick fix" will solve them all. Like the geologic processes of the Earth, which occur so slowly that they seem not to be occurring at all, economic changes, especially in a society as large and wealthy as that of the United States, seem also to be proceeding at a snail's crawl.

Vision for the political process spans a time line of not more than one or two years, for it is incumbent on American politicians to produce results immediately. And it is that way because the political process reflects our own ideas. Even the Index of Leading Economic Indicators, so frequently cited by economists, pretends to tell us what may happen in 12 to 18 months. Ideas that might take 10, 15 or 20 years or longer to evolve and produce benefits are never even suggested. Politicians know that we, as Western thinkers not used to seeing the larger picture, would never cast our votes for such plans. One of the criticisms leveled at U.S. business leaders is that, unlike their Japanese counterparts, they see things only in terms of annual profits. Since the onslaught of Japanese products and their gains in the 1970s and 1980s, and the consequent loss of market shares by

U.S. businesses, some of these long-term thinking processes have begun to sink in. But we are talking here about new ideas that take generations to evolve. The problems we face have been around for eons, yet we expect solutions in a day or a week or during the term of office of an elected politician.

Economic indicator charts show that trends do not simply rise or fall. They zigzag up and down, but over time the direction becomes clear. Our politicians point only to the latest rise or fall, depending upon their need, because both they and our thinking are limited to only the most immediate of benefits or detriments.

Economic imbalance and its consequences come in part because we fail to recognize how our daily lives and the choices we each make affect money and resources. We do not see, or we do not want to see, how these personal choices—choices about the cars we drive, the purchases we make, the attitudes we have about "foreigners" working in "our" country, our long-standing and unquestioned attitudes about money—become extrapolated into national and international finances, politics, and leadership issues. The economic problems we face today are not the result of mysterious forces beyond our control. They come as a result of our personal points of view, which over the years have become transformed into national and international economic policies. We are suffering today because these points of view become translated into politics by our votes or our lack of votes, as well as by our own personal policies about how we spend our money. The fundamental relationships that have created the sizable social cancers of unemployment, poverty, famine, homelessness, greed, and war, all of which are related and all of which seem to have been around since the beginning of recorded history, are the result of the way we define ourselves and our relationship to the world. These points of view have not changed in any significant way.

We do things in the name of "business" that we would never do in our "personal" lives, as though the two were discrete entities. "It's just business," we have all rationalized at one time or another. We believe the concept of a "business" to be actually some separate entity acting independently of those who run it. We tell ourselves it is "the business" that is firing thousands of people, and forget that it is men and women in gray suits who make that decision.[1] It is our "government" that makes war and kills—in our name or under the guise of something called "national security," the meaning of which we have come to believe we actually understand. As a result, we feel comfortable with hurting "the other" since it is not us; it is "Them." Even those who work for "government" act as though they are separate and apart from the rest of us. They speak of "the taxpayer" as an entity divorced from themselves.

We feel no connection to the universe and, therefore, no responsibility for its care. We do not take responsibility for our own conduct. If we vote, we feel it's permissible to complain. If we do not vote, we feel it's permissible to complain. We never question when the line is crossed between individual conduct that is immoral—and the same behavior we consider moral and acceptable if done collectively. We elect leaders who tell us they are ethical but conduct themselves in unethical ways. We sanction that behavior by reelecting them, if by a narrower margin.

The decline of our major businesses as symbols of everlasting security, the overwhelming problems of welfare, poverty, drug abuse, and poor educational achievements are all examples of the results of the economic repression we have exerted over natural forces. The economic imbalance created by these unnatural policies is now beginning to crack under the strain of that repression. It is unfortunate indeed that such a correction will be accompanied by substantial disruption and human suffering, but it is the price we pay for our attempts at repression.

We are living in a time of chaos. Traditional ideas about the way the world operates are no longer valid.

Dominant nations have given way to what were, 25 or so years ago, small, underdeveloped nations. Many of us can remember from childhood the main exports from Japan, straw finger traps and wooden slides that took our pennies; in retrospect, these seem prescient. Nations that were at war for centuries are now joined in economic unions. The dichotomy of two super-powers has become a cacophony of new nations. Not changing as quickly as the times is our resistance to these changes. Our lack of vision keeps us slavishly bound to the past and to now passé concepts that dominated our thinking for centuries. We continue to look to political leaders who promise "change" but who merely perpetuate the old order, albeit with alter-ations at the fringes. We continue to elect ordinary men in extraordinary times.

Wholesale reevaluation of our individual lives is more in line with what we need to be doing; major change, however, especially major change at the per-sonal level, is the most difficult thing we ever have to do. We simply refuse to change, fundamentally change, unless forced to by circumstances seemingly beyond our control. It is, of course, these very cir-cumstances that are really opportunities to rearrange our personal economic lives and points of view, to live more benign lives—and, in the process, to find peace. Peace about money and, in turn, about ourselves. And peace about ourselves can open the possibilities for peace in the world.

We have not merged our inner voices into the entirety of our beings, and so live a dual existence. We do so out of fear. We are not whole inside our minds, and this schism becomes part of our world view. It is time for us to let go and trust in the chaos, for it is only out of the chaos that change can occur. We can now see our problems from a fresh point of view, without preconceived ideas about what will and what will not work—because the world is brand-new. The fundamental changes taking place, creating the insecurity we feel, are the same fundamental changes that have made the world brand-new.

Indeed, because of the chaos of change, this is the time when dreams can come true. To make these dreams reality, however, we will have to discard virtually all of our old concepts. And we will have to do so individually before we can do so collectively.

It is never too late to give up our prejudices. No way of thinking or doing, however ancient, can be trusted without proof. What everybody echoes or in silence passes by as true to-day may turn out to be falsehood to-morrow, mere smoke of opinion, which some had trusted for a cloud that would sprinkle fertilizing rain on their fields. What old people say you cannot do, you try and find that you can.[2]

The problems persist because we have been treating the symptoms and not the disease, thinking all the while that the symptoms are the disease. The disease is a disease of the mind but, like many such diseases, it has taken its toll on the body. Although we must treat the symptoms to take care of our immediate needs, our real energies should be directed toward the causes, so that we cure what ails us for all time. We must simply face the truth: *We* are the causes—we, both collectively and we individually. The proper approach is to change what, inside our minds, causes us to feel and act in the ways we do about money, both directly and indirectly.

Money is used here in the broadest context, not limited to currency and the like. Money is often used as a substitute for self-worth, and how we think about ourselves becomes directly translated into how we spend our money. If we do not love ourselves, for whatever reason, we tend to feel that we can overcome our personal shortcomings by driving gas-guzzling cars; speed and leather replace self-respect and trust. Instead of becoming introspective, we shop.

As we change our minds, our world can change. Change in the human psyche will not come quickly, because the problems that psyche has created will not be solved by some new law or new program or new political leader. Change can never be imposed by something outside of ourselves. It must be felt by each of us, inside.

We have made major progress in science and technology, in the externals of our lives, but the fundamental ideas about our relationship to our selves, to the planet and to everyone on it, have not changed. Today, in this age of a global marketplace with products made everywhere and thus nowhere, we are still fighting over resources and jobs separated by artificial lines. We no longer have to. Today, as the pall of pollution transcends these same imaginary lines, we are still destroying our home and blaming it on the other guy, the one across that artificial line. We no longer have to.

We have not yet spanned the mental and emotional bridges from yesterday to today and, indeed, into tomorrow. We proclaim the coming of the twenty-first century but remain mired in the thinking of the nineteenth. As a result, we are left behind in the dust of yesterday.

We have wonderful capabilities. We have the unequaled ability to create beauty and art and music, and the depth of feeling about ourselves to care about humanity when we see others in need. Not just rational creatures, we are also loving and humane; we are alive.

And yet, we are in a state of supreme denial. Failing to connect the illness with the disease, we do not see how we are causing the very problems we seek to stop. We feel powerless to effect change, in our personal lives and in the collective life of the planet. We feel victims of some great unknown and malefic power and tell ourselves these lies even as we toss candy wrappers from the windows of our cars, and have told ourselves these lies for so long that they have become our truth. As a result, our thinking has atrophied out of despair.

However, it is very difficult to break out of our old habits unless the pain of continuing is too great. As long as that pain is bearable, we persist, fearing the future and the unknown more than we fear the pain, repeating old ideas and patterns in our personal lives.

> Because of our feelings of insecurity, we tend to want to control the world and others in it in our attempt to feel safe. We believe that if we are in control of our world, we will be secure. It never works. But we continue to try, never wanting to admit to ourselves that it is not working, for to do so would mean that all of our perceptions about ourselves, about the universe, would be wrong. It would mean that what we have believed for eons is simply not so. It would be shattering.[3]

On the larger stage, we pursue national and international policies that have created nothing for us except the crises we now face. We pretend we are doing something as we bounce, like a child's multicolored ball, from one major political party to another and then back again, thinking that one is different from the other or that one offers solutions that the other does not.

It appears that the only real election we have made is not to change. We are, consciously or unconsciously, electing to poison our environment. By continuing to build weapons of war and electing to office those who advocate the same, we are choosing war as a means of "solving" our problems, without understanding that we are choosing death as a means of attempting to live. We have failed to learn the life-sustaining connections among the natural forces of the planet, continuing to choose hamburgers over the planet's survival, and technology over protection from the sun's ultraviolet rays. We have elected to spend our money and resources in ways that cause unequal educational opportunities, leading to gangs, drugs, and other forms of destructive behavior.

The problems we face are enormous and pervasive, and in order to deal with them, we need a place to start. Where to begin? Everything is connected to everything else, and there is no way to talk about anything without at the same time talking about everything. There seems virtually no way of solving anything without simultaneously solving everything. It is all a big circle with no end and no place to begin . . . at least it seems that way.

The Tao of Money is one approach to a new way of seeing. This book is about global change coming as a result of personal, individual change. It is about a very old way of thinking that now seems appropriate for today's times. The world is a new place. Significant changes over the past few years, such as the dissolution of the Soviet Union and the rise of new economic and industrial nations, have demanded that we rethink what we have thought for eons before these changes took place.

Taoism, which is based on the *Tao Te Ching*, "the book of the natural or harmonious way," is an ancient Chinese philosophy dating back at least 2,500 years to a philosopher named Lao Tzu. The *Tao Te Ching* consists of 81 aphorisms and sayings and is about seeing the world as a connected, unified whole and allowing the natural forces to prevail. Today, more than ever, just such an approach seems called for, as we have exhausted the traditional solutions. Indeed, it seems that those solutions have turned out to be simply more of the problems. What we need are old ideas for these new times.

The *Tao Te Ching* tells us that we must learn to follow the natural processes that are at work in the universe, in all parts of our individual lives and in our collective lives as nations. By living as close as we can to these natural forces, we will be living in harmony with the universe, and our lives can then be easier and not as forced and coerced as they are today. The Tao tells us that in order to survive, we must feel connected to all of existence, for only then will we not knowingly destroy ourselves. Because the Tao provides us with this unity to everything, it helps us feel secure. Any harm we do, we do to ourselves. Any safety we feel, we feel because we know we are part of the entirety of everything. The Tao keeps us from giving away our power to those we have come to believe are better able to make decisions for us. *We* can solve the problems for ourselves, but first we must see that we *are* the problems.

The *Tao Te Ching* gives us guidelines for personal and, in turn, objective, real-world conduct. In its essence, the Tao tells us to let go of our attempts at controlling the world and the people and ourselves in it, for nothing is controllable. Our attempts at such coercion lead only to frustration and anger, because such conduct is futile. The angrier and more frustrated we get, the more we attempt to control, leading only to more frustration and more anger. By *control*, I mean not just controlling others in our personal lives but controlling other nations and other people living in those nations—by virtue of making war on them as well as through monetary and social programs that keep them under tight rein.

In the second paragraph of this chapter I referred to letting rather than making the world work. This difference runs throughout the ideas I express in this book, and this is the difference that is at the heart of Taoism. From a real-world point of view, the difference means that the solutions about which I speak may require little or no effort or control, on our part or on the part of governments, to be successful. What that also means is that the solutions can be free to find themselves, and that translates in turn into less interference from government and potentially less need for expensive programs to "make" the solutions work. This frees up more money for each of us to have, to improve our lives in the way we choose.

Taoism is a very personal, very subtle approach to behavior, one in which very few of us have any training. It requires that we get very close to our own selves, something that is deeply uncomfortable to many of us. And yet, deep inside our souls, we each know that the essence of the Tao is true. We each know that nature will take its course in everything, no matter how much we lie to ourselves that we are the actors, the creators of our destinies. More importantly, giving ourselves over to a power larger than ourselves enables us to have a totally different understanding about our roles in our own lives and in the life of the planet. It enables us to see events as part of a continuum and so may give us new ideas that would not have become apparent with our more egocentric point of view.

The Tao represents the totality of everything, the sum and substance of the universe. It is God. It tells us that change can lead to completion and balance and harmony, and that our most productive conduct in both our personal lives and that of the world, may be to let change occur naturally, without interference. If we are self-secure enough to let go of our frantic if hopeless attempts to control everyone and everything, if we can have faith in ourselves and in our universe, in God, then we can learn to adapt those spiritual ideas into concrete actions in our daily lives, most particularly when it comes to money. New vistas and new ideas about work, consumption, and value systems can then emerge. We can then use these new ideas in the outer world and, as a result, change the way we look at the world and the way the world looks to us. The world then may have more people living in harmony with it and no longer resisting it. We then have the opportunity to find personal peace, and then world peace.

In a pragmatic sense, the Tao mirrors the state of our monetary world today. With products made everywhere, there is no separation between peoples and nations. With information transmitted instantly around the globe, and into and back from outer space, with television providing immediate access to events anywhere on the planet, traditional borders are eliminated and we are an integrated, unified whole. The world today is a single unit, both socially and economically, and Taoism tells us that is so. Taoism tells us that we are connected to everything in a spiritual sense, while the "real world" tells us that is so in concrete terms.

> Connectivity rather than disconnectedness, integration rather than disintegration, real-time simultaneity rather than sequential stages— these are the assumptions that underlie the new production paradigm.[4]

The *Tao Te Ching* can give us unlimited choices. By helping us to live free of fear, it can open up options that never before were apparent. That which will be, will be. If we can absorb this, we can be free of the constraints that have kept us bound up tightly for all of our lives. As a vehicle for this process of change, the Tao is a natural. It cuts across all issues: political, such as war and peace; personal, such as love and control; social, such as poverty, wealth, and economics; ecological, such as pollution and destruction of our home environment. The Tao deals with the fundamental relationships at the heart of these issues that are killing us all. The Tao is nonreligious, although it directly relates to spirituality and God. You will note that I frequently use the terms Tao, God, and the universe more or less synonymously. I believe that nature itself and all its processes are creations of God. I also use the term God nonreligiously, referring to the entirety of everything—the universe and, in turn, the Tao. Taoism can offend no one except those who are closed to the new. The Tao directs us inward. Once we see ourselves in relation to the "problem," the solution may become easy.

The Tao however, is not a panacea. Neither it nor this book are plans of action or blueprints for change. Both are merely tools for guidance. *The Tao of Money* is not about how to get a better job, or how to invest wisely, or how to earn more money. Those results may flow when we come to understand our connection to economic and monetary events taking place "out there" and then see how we may adapt that understanding to our own lives. The Tao is only one such tool among a host of others; taken together, they can be used by each of us to effectuate change in our personal lives. The Tao is not absolutist: Following the natural way can mean, under any given set of circumstances, various things. The "rules" of the Tao, like those of nature itself, are flowing and in constant change. This, of course, makes for less-than-simple answers, which is a less-than-acceptable arrangement for most of us. We crave certainty even at the risk of perpetuating the problem.

And so you must use the Tao in a way that works within your own life as well as in the life of our planet. The suggestions I make in this book are only ideas about how to apply Taoist ideas in concrete terms. But they are only suggestions, the broad strokes; the details are up to you.

I have chosen to focus on money because money and its consequences are at the heart of virtually every other social issue. War is almost always about money and power, which are frequently synonymous. Hence, I have used the term *warmoneywar* to describe this connection. As long as we have war, we cannot have peace. War is so much about money and vested interests that to discuss peace without discussing economics seems futile. Money is also what separates people (those who have it from those who do not). I do not advocate doing away with money or possessions or private property, but merely attempt to show how money's use without social awareness has been part of the problem.

Of necessity, the processes involved in changing our concepts about money, on both an individual level and then on a global scale, must involve discussions of personal growth. To be able to let go, to be able to trust, to be able to become one with the planet, to be able to have faith and apply those ideas to the hard realities of realpolitik—all require great personal strength and development.

Some of what I suggest in this book may seem radical or naive. But instead of judging those ideas on the basis of our current points of view, we must let go of those points of view and trust in ourselves enough to try something new. Or old. The reason I chose to frame these concepts in Taoist thought is because they take us down to the most fundamental—yes, simple—of all principles: that we must learn to live in harmony and balance with our surroundings if we are to survive. In terms of money, we must learn to use money in ways that do not destroy but rather create, ways that do not harm but rather nurture.

To be able to let go of all of the forces of coercion we have developed since the beginning of time and live with harmony on a global scale, we must first grow secure enough within ourselves to do so on an individual level. By letting go of control and trusting in our individual lives, we can begin to see how new national and international points of view can be developed. The Tao teaches that we are all part of the same universality; as a result, it is not "we here" and the rest of the world "out there," floating on the ether, as it were. What we can achieve in our individual lives might be achieved by nations just as well.

The world is, after all, nothing but all of us added up.

Principle 1:
The World Is Only All of Us Added Together

The "money" problems that confront us in our daily lives can, if not checked and handled on our individual levels, become blended into the problems faced by the world in general. As we go through these crises, how we deal with them may teach us not only about ourselves but about how we and our points of view fit into the larger set of issues, of which we are all a part.

In a sense, it is our collective failure to return one another's telephone calls that is, at the roots, the cause of monetary chaos, war, and self-destruction. We all seem to be on the verge of exploding, though most of us vent our anger in socially acceptable ways. We choose to act more subtly but equally effectively. But the insecurities and fears and frustrations inside of us are boiling just below our peaceful facades. Given the slightest reason, we take out these frustrations on others in ways society has come to accept as normal.

People who do not like themselves and their own images turn that dislike outside themselves and onto others. We treat others in the way we feel we have been treated in our lives, whether or not those feelings are true. If we feel we are unworthy, we treat others as though they are unworthy. When, for example, we get upset with the telephone company in the person of a clerk, or the bank in the person of the teller, rather than recognizing the source of our frustration and empathizing with our collective plight, we vent this frustration on that other person, and they do the same. Their need to maintain their job is more important than the underlying moral principles. That belief makes them defend the "system" that is equally oppressive to all of us. And our response to their conduct makes us behave similarly. Each of us is trying to out "Oh! Yeah?!" the other.

When we treat one another discourteously by, for example, not returning telephone calls, we are passing along our own ill feelings. What we are really saying to one another is, "I am angry at the world. I am not in control of the world. I cannot do anything about much of this lack of control, so I will take it out on you by attempting to exercise control over you." This sort of conduct leads to increased frustration in the recipient of your conduct and that recipient inevitably passes that frustration along to someone else, who does the same. And, like the childhood game of "Telephone," what starts out at 9:00 A.M. as one thing, by 5:00 P.M. becomes you yelling at other drivers on the freeway going home.

We deny to others that which we have denied to ourselves. If we are not free, we fear giving others the right to be free. Instead, we must regard ourselves as the source of all power and weakness, and not divorce ourselves from the consequences of our conduct by relegating our actions to the machinations of some "system," the mythical "them." The world is a consequence of what each of us is. How the world behaves is an aggregation of how each of us behaves. We are the universe, and it is us.

We like to think of ourselves as separated from this process. But it is well to remember that

> Cruelty has a Human Heart,
> And Jealousy a Human Face;
> Terror the Human Form Divine,
> And Secrecy the Human Dress.[1]

This separation causes us to see the world in a dualistic fashion, "us" versus "them," the "them" defined variously depending upon the situation. It can be another nation, another interest group, the poor, the elderly, another race, and so on. This point of view leads inevitably toward a need to control the "them" so that we may feel more secure. However, when the source of our insecurities lies outside of ourselves, we can never be secure—for we know that we do not truly have control over anything outside of ourselves. We like to believe we do, but when we go to sleep at night, when (if ever) we tell ourselves the truth, we know we do not have this control. And because we know this truth, instead of dealing with it appropriately by learning more about ourselves, we try to exert even greater control over those outside forces.

Taoism is about trying to return to the original connection to the universe with which we were born. This is our connection to the entirety of everything and is the essence of Taoism. By doing less, we can achieve more, because our conduct may not be interfering with the forces of nature. Doing less means being able to exert minimal efforts toward achieving our goals, and we can only do this by *using* the natural forces instead of confronting them. In the context of economic and other social policies, it means letting them find their own level instead of trying to coerce them.

Applying this to our daily lives, in which we deal with money and economics, means that we must learn to use money in a way that harmonizes with our lives and the lives of everyone else. For many of us, however, money has become a means of exerting power and control over others. Instead of using money to achieve peace, we are using it to create division. As we will explore later on, we are using money to harm, and we are doing so because it reflects our personal point of view about ourselves.

Each of us plays a part in this process, by virtue of our fear-based points of view as well as our personal economic decisions. For example, we are a credit card-based economy, and being in debt leads to massive insecurity. Being afraid to lose our jobs, houses, and careers is bad enough, but when these fears are compounded by the need to earn a certain amount each month to pay off our debts, we are led to compromise our standards, our ethics, our morals, our very selves—just to maintain the fiction which is our house of credit. Because we can see no alternative, we find ourselves "trapped" in jobs we dislike. We hate going to work and this hatred becomes part of our outer-world viewpoint: We yell at other drivers and treat others discourteously because we are unfulfilled.

This is one of our connections to "the system." This individual pressure not only ratifies our view that there is something to fear, but gives life to it. It is the reason why those fears seem real. We have to fear anyone who threatens our ability to live on credit or lose it all. So we fear the immigrants who are seeking low-paying work. We fear another country's cars or computers or pasta, because we think they threaten our own employment. We fear anything that feeds our insecurities, and then this fear gets translated into votes for politicians who themselves fear and who pander to our fears. When those politicians propose restrictions on immigration or imports, it rings true to us, and so we go along with those programs.

Doing less, on the other hand, might translate into a simpler life style, one involving not so much restriction and pressure. More on this in a bit.

Our internal value systems about money determine our external conduct. If we believe money exists simply to buy us things, then we will place greater emphasis on things: fancy cars, huge houses, excessive consumption. If we use money to reward or punish our children or our employees, we condone such conduct in the world at large, in the form of tariffs against goods made elsewhere and immigration laws to keep out "economic refugees." That money represents security is a valid viewpoint, but if coupled with this idea we feel pressure to continue to do work we dislike because we earn security doing so, rather than seeking to change that work, then our global point of view may be skewed. It becomes opposed to anything new or different, for new and different equals change, and change equals fear and uncertainty.

Money *can* bring security—but only if we are secure within ourselves in the first place. Otherwise, the same amount of money can cause great fear and insecurity. If we are insecure enough we are willing to significantly compromise our standards and values to achieve that security. When money brings no pleasure to us, then it is, in fact, being used to harm, not heal. And if we gain no pleasure from money ourselves, we may not be adverse to using money to harm others.

If, on the other hand, we value more spiritual, personal ideals when it comes to money, then we may place greater emphasis on openness and sharing, and that may lead, for example, to free immigration without controls, or no economic restrictions on trade. We would probably not see economic enemies and might consequently find no need to restrict and control others with our money and the power that we think it brings.

By using money to trick ourselves into believing we are better persons, we may then need ever more expensive and probably useless goods to prove it to the world. We never seem to understand that the more we acquire, the less secure we generally feel, for we are always in fear of losing these things. If we learn, however, that we are whole, secure, loving people, if we develop a greater faith in God, in trusting in the Tao, in the universe, then we can reduce our consumption significantly, for we know that wealth does not determine who we are. We are not our things; losing or giving up our things is not losing or giving up ourselves. Ironically, of course, the more we acquire in order to prove our worthiness to ourselves, the more we may fear that people like us merely for those things, and so the less secure we may truly feel. Stripped to the bone, we might be just be valued for ourselves alone: That truth scares the hell out of most of us, because we do not believe in that kind of worthiness.

Once we examine our personal economic situations and do whatever we can to gain freedom from our troubling value systems, it may enable us to look at economic policies, both personal and on the larger scale, free of those constraints. When he was president, Jimmy Carter, at the height of the inflation that saw the prime rate skyrocket, said that Americans should refrain from using credit cards when they could. Following that suggestion may have saved significant money for many people who didn't have much cash in their pockets. It is credit card debt that significantly contributes to personal insecurity, since it is credit card debt that most affects our personal lives.

Returning to the examples I mentioned at the beginning of this chapter, it is clear we take our personal fears out on everyone we touch, in business as well as in our personal world. Being in debt has, I am certain, been the source of much divorce and family disruption, which are but steps in what seems to be an inexorable process leading to separation from others, mistrust of others, and a willingness to accept others as enemies. That allows us to justify to ourselves the fatality of war and economic repression as recourses to our problems.

We need to see fear as part of the larger picture, for it is fear that brought us to where we are today. Fear has led to economic policies that have brought us major recession and economic disruption. We live, collectively, with a huge national debt. In large part, that debt has come about because of spending on war, and war represents fear. Today's significant economic problems, if those problems can for the moment be isolated from their social counterparts, are due in great degree to this vast national debt. Money is removed from productive use to pay both interest and principal on that debt, which is held by a very small number of people, here and in other nations. A very large portion of our national (hence personal) money burden goes simply to satisfy this debt. More on this later, too. Living with large personal debt leads to loss of integrity and lack of freedom. Living with large national debt does the same. Both lead to the fear of

something, someone, some nation outside, controlling us. Our notion that we have some sort of right to
continued acquisition, even in the face of what we are
doing to our world, our personal as well as global
world, leads us to try to control the world of money.

A reordering of personal priorities is called for.
To achieve this, each of us individually must examine
his or her own consumption and spending patterns,
for what we see on the larger scale is only each of our
own individual demands and needs, multiplied by
everyone else's. Many of us have replaced feelings with
consumption, thinking that the more we have the
better we are. So we want more and more, and the
more and more we get, the more and more we need,
because getting more and more does not satisfy our
emptiness. So we go after bigger, more gas-consuming
cars, spend more on things that set us apart from
others, and get trapped in this never-ending cycle.

There is an unexpected reason all these things are
called possessions: *They* possess *us*. In reality, personal
growth and freedom from fear are integrally connected to *reduction* of consumption. Simpler living,
and more flexibility with changes in our personal economic conditions, may help to give us peace. Reordering our priorities can give us the flexibility not to feel
pressured into making moral and ethical compro-
mises about our work, about freedom for others, and

such—all of which lower our standards and cause us in turn to make real-world decisions that mirror those lowered standards. We must make the courageous decision to honestly question ourselves about what money and the things it can buy really mean to us. Do we use money to define ourselves, both to ourselves and to others? Do we feel comfortable about what is meaningful to us when we know these definitions depend upon externals to give them meaning? Are we dissatisfied enough to want to change?

> The world is too much with us; late
> and soon,
>
> Getting and spending, we lay waste
> our powers:
>
> Little we see in Nature that is
> ours;[2]

Wordsworth tells us that when it comes to money, we fail to connect ourselves with the rest of the planet. "The world" is the outer world. It gets in the way of "us," meaning our inner world, and becomes more important than that inner world. We defer our personal lives to it, to money, to "getting and spending," and in doing so, we deplete ourselves of creativity and energy. Because "Little we see in Nature that is ours;" we fail to understand that everyone's economic survival depends upon everyone else's.

Living simply does not mean doing without, but rather examining our "needs" to see if they are really "needs" and our "wants" to see how they affect others elsewhere, as well as the planet as a whole. Excessive consumption creates forces of repression that are designed to protect us from losing what we have consumed, which keep things out of balance. We try to protect our "American standard of living" by depriving people in other nations of the right to their standard of living. We do this, for example, by restricting the right of those people to sell their goods in our country, because if they did so, it might cause a loss of "American" jobs. We impose tariffs against those goods to protect ourselves, never understanding —or if understanding, never caring—what effects those barriers have on "the other."

This excessive consumption sometimes may be related not only to whatever emotional insecurity we have developed in our lives but to the duality inherent in our separateness from the universe. If we learn to see ourselves instead as connected to everyone and everything else, as the Tao suggests, then we may learn that our work must be something we "are" rather than something we "do." We have created a dualism in terms of this work. We do this or that Monday through Friday, but we do what we *like* to do only on the weekends or in our spare time. Learning that work must be "heart-felt," and that the heart is where God reposes, means our work will be what we enjoy doing, and that work must, in some sense, contribute to the well-being of others, or at the very least, not harm others.

Our personal struggle must be to find out what God intended for us to be doing in this lifetime—a difficult task at best. When we can earn money with both our hearts as well as our heads, when we no longer see our business life as disconnected from our personal life, we may find that our level of frustration abates considerably, thereby lessening the tension and hostility we project into the world, and reducing our vulnerability to the convincing arguments that we must war against the enemy.

For many of us, it is difficult to make these changes, and extreme changes may, indeed, not be necessary. Learning to become "present" in our work, learning not to resent the work (because resentment implies that we are not "present" or that we are wishing we were doing something else), may be the answer. Focusing on the moment, almost in a meditative state, may enable us to appreciate the work we are doing. Instead of changing our work, we can change our minds. Watch professional athletes, and notice their extreme concentration on their work. To be successful, they must block out any thoughts beyond the immediate moment.

At this point, I am certain that many of you will say this change is impossible to achieve. It is not. It is difficult, but it is not impossible. It takes a deep and challenging examination of ourselves, our value systems, our beliefs, our faiths—but it is not impossible. It takes careful financial planning if part of the decision involves changing careers; it takes giving up excessive spending, but it is not impossible. It takes believing that the gnawing sensation we feel about our work is God telling us it is time to stop repressing our natural instincts. Letting go of that repression may create disruption, very much like letting go of the world's financial repression is creating disruption. But if it is a choice to cease doing meaningless work that disrupts your peace of mind, work that makes you part of the larger problem and keeps you from living closer to your heart, the choice is really no choice at all. Once we are personally fulfilled in terms of our work, which is so much about who we are, we may find ways of looking at world "problems" that we did not see before. We may be willing to see possibilities in solutions that before seemed impossible.

> Work, done rightly, affords the individual an understanding of the key principles of life and of the universe, and—moreover—that work is a critical avenue and a discipline for personality health and optimum, responsible functioning.[3]

I do not mean that everyone should give up their immediate work. All I am suggesting is that we must dig deeply into our souls to discover what we are supposed to be doing as work in this lifetime, for it is only when we find that heart sign that we can be fulfilled in our work. And it is when we are fulfilled in our work that we may be able to become open to new ideas that require letting go of old, rigid concepts about money. Until then, our fear of change, which is rooted in our personal insecurities and which may take the form of overanxious concerns about money, may keep us from seeing the world in a new fashion, where abundance, not scarcity, is the norm.

Where Does Our Fear Come From?

From birth we are taught scarcity, and that scarcity shows up in diverse forms. Many of these do not even look like scarcity but have scarcity as their root: scarcity about love, about losing, about fearing, and about seeing the world with those limits in mind.

Since we are talking about money, let me give just one example. Many of us come from parents and grandparents who lived during the Great Depression, or who migrated to the U.S. from the poverty of Eastern Europe. They learned, from bitter experience, that not having money was terrible. The corollary, that having money is wonderful, though not necessarily following from the original idea, was what they taught us. And so we learned early on to go after the money, for in the money, we were told, we would find security. It was not true then, nor is it true today. Yet we continue on the same path of chasing the dollar in the name of security. It is not the money that creates security, but the mind, and if we still have scarcity in our minds, all the money in the world will not make us secure.

Scarcity leads inevitably to a lack of self-worth. If We have something, then we believe that someone must lack that same thing, since scarcity tells us there is only a finite amount of anything to go around. And if They have, we believe that We must lack. As a result, we are constantly having to be vigilant that we do not lose our things, translated into our selves and our values. And so we end up not trusting our true worth, which is internal and abundant.

This lack of self-worth, which comes from the early stages of life, perpetuates itself in many forms in our adult lives and also permeates our world view. The most obvious of these viewpoints is that the world is full of enemies, economic as well as military, and if we have enemies, we must have economic and military war. But "enemies" are not limited to people in other countries. That same term is implied, if not expressed, when we fear that satisfying the needs of others will deprive us of some corresponding benefit. As a result, we operate out of fear. We perpetuate old, no longer relevant ideas about the world, including the world of money and our relationship to it, out of this fear. Better to be certain, if mistaken, than to let go of the certain mistake in favor of the uncertain "who knows?"

It takes no great leap of imagination to go from childhood insecurities and the fear of being out of control of our world, to adulthood insecurities and the fear of being out of control now, too. That which we learned as children is simply applied to new situations as adults, however much out of place it may be in our current lives.

Depending upon your age, you may remember the day in your early childhood education when you began to study world geography. Your teacher reached up to the top of the blackboard and pulled down a multicolored map of the world. You were young and impressionable, and the map-maker's interpretation, when reinforced by the teacher, probably made an indelible and lasting impression. There, in the absolute dead center of everything, was the United States of America. Off center of us were Canada and Alaska, the latter not yet a state in the early fifties, and toward the bottom, beneath us as it were, lay Mexico, Central America, and South America. Across the Atlantic Ocean and toward the schoolyard window stretched Europe and Asia, including part of the Union of Soviet Socialist Republics. On the opposite side of the map, toward the wall, beyond the Pacific, was the other part of Asia, including Japan and China and the balance of the U.S.S.R. The United States of America was always colored a nice shade of green, and the U.S.S.R. was a shade of pink. (This was the fifties, after all.) I am certain that children in other countries, as well, had maps that made their nation the center of the world.

Given that many of our political leaders today grew up in the fifties or before, those early learning experiences have left their mark upon their collective world view and, in turn, on the social and political policies determined by that view and with which we are dealing today. None of those leaders had the benefit children have today of seeing the planet from space. Once we understand that in reality there is no up, no down, no center, and no side, once we see that there are no lines, it should all turn around in our minds. But my generation and earlier ones did not have and were not taught that point of view, and first impressions are the longest-lived.

As a result of this sort of experience, our world view is that we in the U.S. are the geographic, economic, and political center of the world, and that view guides us today. As long as that point of view coincided with our seeming reality, as in the post-World War II era and into the early 1970s, we felt comfortable and self-assured. But that same world view is today the source of much of our anger and frustration and consequent real-world responses as we see our imagined position slipping. That conduct takes the form of wars, both killing and economic, to protect this ideal with which we grew up. When Copernicus proposed that the Earth was not the center of the universe, hundreds of years passed before that "new" idea was accepted, because it conflicted with everything taught before.

In the universe that is implied from the old map of the world, we may imagine that there is an enemy "out there," separate and apart from us. No one questions that premise because, in fact, there are wars and there is killing. There are jobs being "lost" to labor in other countries, and so the premise seems verified by "real-world" events. But no one asks *who* the enemy is, *what* the goal of the supposed enemy is, or *how* the enemy is going to achieve this goal. On a more fundamental level, we have grown to believe that we understand what constitutes this "nation" we are protecting. No one asks whether, to accompany our more modern and more enlightened point of view about what the world looks like, we should have a new set of ideas to deal with this new vision. Instead, like dutiful robots, we march in lockstep to a tune that is out of touch with reality but, because it is reinforced by our conduct and our personal beliefs, convinces us that it is the only true reality. To believe otherwise would be, and is, today's heresy, much as were the new ideas of Copernicus.

Once we erase the lines, from our minds and from the map, the world is an integrated unit. But we have lived with lines for so long that they seem to us real. We could go back to the beginning of recorded history to see where lines came from. We could blame the whole thing on the ancient Sumerians, who, between 5,000 and 3,000 B.C., inhabited the area around the Tigris and Euphrates rivers in what was then called Mesopotamia and is now Iraq. It was these people who, to a great extent, developed the early versions of agriculture and commerce.

As a result of the societal changes developed by the Sumerians, land and animals had to be fenced to protect ownership. Property was divided instead of held in common. The Earth was no longer there for the survival of all; instead, individuals depended upon their own property to stay alive, unless they could trade with others who had what was needed. Over time, as more and more landowners and animal owners congregated, communities were formed from the separate holdings of each individual and family. Each such community then took on the responsibility of protecting the farms and holdings of its members from those of the next community, and each community developed its own separateness from the others.

As the communities formed, they combined into larger units for efficiency and collective defense against other such combinations of communities. These combinations of communities in turn became towns, and towns became larger towns, cities, states, and nations. Each such unit was separated from other units of its kind by the same divisions that originally separated the individual farms from one another.

The rest, as they say, is history. The lines drawn on the map were constantly changing, based on who won the last conflict. Instead of everyone sharing the collective whole, everyone protected their own. Humanity, collectively, made a Mesopotamia.

The schoolroom example is appropriate in another way. Past and present teaching methods school us to look for "the" answer: Choose *a*, *b*, or *c*. "All of the above" presents problems for many of us. The "answer" to any given problem is usually not one of a multiple choice but rather an essay, which requires us to examine many alternative solutions without, in many cases, coming up with a clear and single answer. But we have come to expect that our politicians will pass a law, restrict imports, or do some specific thing to solve "the" problem. Today no candidate to office gets elected without a concrete set of proposals to deal with everything. The nature of the Tao is that it may give us the confidence to proceed into this otherwise murky realm of "no answer," but just try to win an election on such a platform.

When our preconceived ideas clash with the observable information, we face a dilemma: Do we adhere to our ideas and either ignore or twist the facts to suit our mold? Or do we discard them and adapt? Our response may depend upon how flexible we are about ourselves and how much we trust in our abilities to accept change as a natural process. This problem affects individuals as well as institutions, such as governments, but the latter, because of their commitment to maintenance of the status quo, are inevitably less likely to move toward acceptance of fundamental change. Those institutions are run by many of us who may be within ourselves unwilling to change, and so the institution fails to change. Institutions are made up of numerous individuals, each of whom carries his or her own individual inertia.

We come to believe that, by accepting established concepts, we are thinking about something—but we are completely shut down. New ideas that conflict with our model are rejected. We allow our political leaders to lie to us, even though we know full well that they are lying. And when they make their election promises, we elect them anyway, even though we know they are lying. We choose those promises we know are lies but want to believe.

Not long ago, a group of voters sought to have an election overturned because they claimed the winning candidate lied during the campaign; had the public known the truth, the voters contended, the winner might not have won. The Senate Rules Committee rejected the claim—not because it was unfounded, but saying, in part, that if allowed, it might lead to the overturning of nearly all elections, thereby implying that lying is part of every campaign. We have institutionalized political deception, as though it were part of the "American way."

We seek support for our world view. If we search diligently enough, we can surely find such support because, as we all know, truth is mutable, even though in our quest we deem it unchanging. We ignore those bits of information which conflict with our viewpoints and, if we have the power to do so, like governments and such, we change those facts to suit our needs.

The Tao and Personal Responsibility

Because we can find comfort in the fact that many of our fellow citizens are as misguided as we are by our political leaders, we feel secure because of the numbers. That we are all paralyzed, unable to evolve into any sort of higher level of being, does not enter into our consideration, and the failure of nearly every one of the social and economic ideas with which we have been living for eons goes unnoticed. We are willing to believe and ignore the realities we face.

The millions of us who make up this comforting crowd, and the political leaders who have led us, have no workable solutions to the real issues we face: economic dislocation; war; pollution; drugs, gangs, and no educational opportunities for millions of youth; lack of food for millions of families. What our politicians tell us rings hollow, and yet, for most of us, it rings true. They campaign for office promising one thing and, when elected, do just the opposite. And we, because we collectively lack enough self-worth to loudly scream and protest, obediently go along with the program because we are afraid to trust our own ideas. Well, we are told, we will simply defeat the enemy wherever they are (and even where they are not). We will censor the press so that word of our failures cannot be spread far and wide and, in doing so, wake a few of us up to the unreality of our reality. From the billions we spend for killing, we will take ridiculously few dollars and allocate them to the living.

We are all waiting for the easy solution, the pat phrase, the one-word answer. We continually look to political leaders who are incapable of an original thought, who rehash what has been rehashed for centuries, with the current results all we have to show for this approach. To say, as the Tao says, that we must approach our problems in a unified way, communicating with those who have been our enemies, with fresh insights, is unacceptable or even unthinkable for most of us. To assume that we can, collectively, unite and end hunger and economic dislocation by a change of the mind is unfathomable to most of us. To combine the resources that the Earth provides in abundance toward health, shelter, and progress for everyone is anathema to those who see us as inevitably divided.

In order to accept ideas that radically alter the way the world operates, we must first be secure enough within ourselves to accept change. What we have held onto for eons has become so ingrained as to seem innate, but it must be questioned because it has not worked. There is significant abundance to share, but we have not yet learned to see it. It requires a deep and abiding inner faith that we will be safe if we follow our instincts, our hearts. It requires a belief that God wants us to evolve, to grow, and that if we move in that direction, we will be enabled with the power to achieve our destinies. (I addressed this notion, which I called the *process of our lives*, more fully in *The Tao of Love* and so will not delve into it more here.)

Once we get to this point in our lives, we then must see how to apply this personal spirituality in the real world. We must see how our ideas—about money, for example—are now being manifested in that world and how we might go about changing them. We must be willing to face our own lack of self-worth, which has been an integral part of bringing us to this point in the first place. We cannot expect to elect officials who advocate the total elimination of war until we first find ourselves at peace. We cannot expect business leaders to stop destroying in the name of profit until we first learn that profit for one may amount to loss for another, and the only true profit is one in which everyone's self-interest is satisfied. I shall present some specific ideas later about how to apply these concepts to "reality."

Just One Example of How the World Is Only Us

Several centuries ago, the world managed to wean itself of its heavy dependance upon indigo, thereby ending Spain's monopoly over this once valuable commodity. The world—We—had a chance to learn a similar lesson in the 1970s and 1980s. During the first oil "crisis"—a crisis only because we were unprepared to accept the situation and the process of change that it entailed—we had the chance to grow less dependent upon the very set of circumstances that we faced again in Iraq/Kuwait in 1990 and 1991, and which became Gulf War I. The most important teaching tool continues to be crisis, both in our individual lives as well as in world affairs, yet we failed to learn from it.

During much of the twentieth century, Americans—indeed much of the industrialized world—grew complacent, smug, and thoughtless of the insecurity and powerlessness arising from our dependency upon an "outside" source for a major resource. In the United States, we were Number One, always had been, and why would it ever be any other way? We forget that many nations—Rome, Greece, Spain, Portugal, and so on—were preeminent through the centuries by controlling whatever was then the valuable commodity. Indeed, Portugal's power was so great that she divided the New World between herself and Spain in the 1500s.

After oil prices skyrocketed in 1973 and rose again in 1979, we began the process of developing energy efficiency. With the rise in oil prices, alternative forms of energy development were potentially profitable within the free market. It seemed possible to develop plans for conservation. Fuel efficiency in automobiles was the chief reason why the then-unknown Japanese automobile industry grew to a position of such dominance. We held the possibilities for energy self-sufficiency within our own hands, and we let those possibilities slip away on the slick of oil. Needless to say, it took the crisis of those oil price increases to coerce us into conservation in the first place.

When the "crisis" passed, it passed only because we became used to gasoline priced over $1.00 per gallon. We grew accustomed to higher prices for food, clothing, plastic, and nearly everything else made from petroleum (which is nearly everything). We fell back into the allure of high-speed, turbo-charged, V6 and V8, 0-to-60 in 7.0 seconds cars. We lost the will to conserve. What this tells us, of course, is that Detroit is not stuffing gas-guzzlers down our throats, but rather we are demanding such cars to satisfy our appetites or our insecurities, and supply has simply gone along with that demand. It is We, not They, who are at fault here. We are exerting forces of control on the world, and those forces cause us to act in other forceful ways in order for us to maintain that control.

We were told during the 1980s that, due to the declining (read stabilizing) price of oil, further exploration of alternative energies was no longer profitable. When we had an opportunity to continue the development of these alternative energies, we squandered it on the foolishness of MX missiles, B-1 bombers, cruise missiles, and Trident nuclear submarines. These weapons were and remain the real-world manifestations of our attempts at control. We built them to maintain our strength over the (then) Soviet Union, to keep them out of the Middle East, among other places, so that we could control the oil and satisfy our unnatural demand for it.

It was the role of responsible government, "us," to subsidize research into the development of alternative energies if market prices did not hold. There are times when it is the responsibility of government to create demand, so that the operation of the free market can get started when it would not have otherwise (more on this later). It is the role of government to seed the system, prime the pump, if you will. Thus it was the responsibility of government, when oil prices fell to the point where it was unprofitable to explore alternatives, to subsidize the marketplace so that such alternatives could be developed. Government does this all the time—for example, when it subsidizes the development of weapons for which there is no marketplace, or when it buys surplus agricultural products.

Instead of building bombs, we should have been aiding in the development and building of solar- or electric-powered automobiles. Instead of telling us of the threat from the Soviets, our government should have been thinking about how to make the nation secure from the need for energy from "external" sources. That should have been government's priority; that, however, required vision.

We might have made a problem—that of our excessive need for oil—into a nonproblem, a very Taoist response, thereby eliminating the need to go to war over it. At the same time, we might have defused the power over us held by nations in the Middle East, a power held over the world even today. The invasion of Kuwait by Iraq was certainly wrong and certainly to be denounced, but were oil not so precious to us, that invasion would not have been a sufficient reason to kill others. In truth, by reducing our own dependence on oil, individually and collectively, we would have made the need to go to war much less significant, and perhaps made it less likely for Iraq to invade Kuwait. As a power lever, the oil would have become as useless as indigo.

In all of these ways, our government let us down. In all of these ways, we let ourselves down. We chose to buy the gas-guzzlers. We chose to elect those who gave only lip service to alternative energies. We failed to insist on change. We wanted to return to what we perceived, in our blindness, to be our glory days. We felt then that we could have it all again, without compromise, without changing the standards to which we had grown accustomed. We were still living as though our schoolroom map of the world were true. Ebb and flow, power and recession, are part of the natural order of things. It is the ebbing that creates the opportunities for a flow, and vice versa. It is the continuum of *yin* and *yang*. When it is flowing, we seem to be able to flow with it, but when it begins to ebb, we reach out, trying to regain that which we had before.

Since the 1980s, we in the United States have substantially increased our importation of oil. A large percentage of the oil our nation consumes each day goes for transportation. There is no clearer example that the They we feared would control our destinies is We ourselves.

Conservation, renewable sources of energy, living more simply and closer to the natural processes of the Earth are examples of doing less and achieving more. Such behavior gives us less reason to fear an outside force, because that force's attempts at controlling a particular resource are no longer a threat to us. These are Taoist solutions in nature because they allow us to be secure without resort to excessive coercive means.

Had we followed the teachings of the Tao, had we been able to feel connected with the entirety of the planet, then our excessive consumption of fuel might not have occurred. We could have been able to live within our consumption means, and Iraq's invasion of Kuwait might not have occurred at all. Living small is the greatest security, but living small does not mean living without. It simply means reordering our priorities, rethinking our needs. But we failed to think. We failed to have politicians with vision, because no one asked for them.

We were seeing the process of change taking place before our very eyes and, just as in our individual lives, we were (and are) unable to cooperate with change and chose instead to fight and resist it. So we went to war. It was the masculine image, not Kuwait, that needed vindication. Our national masculine image—the United States as Number One—had been shaken by a smaller nation. We had had enough. We acted as automatons, unthinking robots. We never thought for ourselves. We were told that if Iraq controlled the Kuwaiti and possibly the Saudi oil fields, we would again have lines at gas stations. What we did not remember was that we had those gas lines when

Kuwait, Saudi Arabia, and others controlled those same oil fields. So we went to war to protect the very nations who originally held us hostage and gave us the gas lines in the first instance!

The way we see the world today is directly contrary to that espoused by the Tao. Our current point of view teaches us that men (read the U.S.) control, and women (read here "lesser" nations) are to be dominated. Men are separate from women. Strong nations are separate from weaker ones. To consider that the stronger nations are in fact dependent upon the weaker ones is unspeakable. That all the nations of the globe make up the entity known as the Earth is only theory; in practice, separateness rules.

There are, of course, many other similar examples of Them being Us. When we fail to provide educational opportunities for those who cannot afford to pay; when people have to drop out of school and we collectively lament our loss of skill competitiveness in world markets and the decline of test scores in our schools; when we fail to see the connections between racial bias and bigotry and the riots that result; when all of this spills over into our cities and our neighborhoods—We and They merge, even if We are unwilling to see it. All this reflects our personal points of view and eventually becomes reflected on the larger stage.

If, therefore, we are to see the economic implications of our belief systems, we must go deep within our souls and see how we create the outer-world manifestations of our inner-world psyches.

Principle 2:
Our Need for Control
Controls Us

We often see stories on the news about (or perhaps we even know some) young "white-collar" workers suddenly finding themselves unemployed for the first time in their lives—no money coming in and none in the bank. Nothing in their backgrounds prepared them for this emotional and monetary trauma. Perhaps they felt they were always going to have secure jobs and careers. In the past few years, all of those idealist notions have fallen by the wayside. Jobs are being displaced—some, as in the men's arm-garter business, never to return again.

These folks are not merely statistics, however; they are real people suffering in real ways. But real people tend to get lost in the computer printouts that conglomerate A generates after its merger with conglomerate B when it has to evaluate the corporate bottom line. Nor perhaps do any of the people in gray suits consider how their decision to let go several thousand employees might affect those individuals and their families. Do any of the laid-off employees have any savings? What about their health care? What about the toll of joblessness on others? Might there be a connection to other social issues, such as alcoholism and heart disease? How does being unemployed affect men whose societal standards have always equated men with money?

Yes, of course it is true that business must turn a profit in order to survive. But it is the way that profit is made and the social consequences it brings that are important. If people in business considered themselves part of the human community before they considered themselves businessmen and women, if they considered themselves to be connected even to those they employ, then perhaps they might alter their decisions. Developing a consciousness of how our individual decisions might impact on others, learning to see ourselves in a larger context, is what is at stake. It is difficult to be more specific here, because each decision must be evaluated on its own merit. Is the merger necessary? Is it going to produce anything more by way of social importance than the nonmerged firm would have? Or is the merger simply about increasing profits for profits' sake?

But, more importantly, how does losing a job change the individual standing alone? Depending upon their level of personal growth, as well as other factors, the newly unemployed might have opportunities to see the circumstances that broke them down as a chance for personal reevaluation. They could decide that God, the universe, was perhaps sending them a message, giving them a strong, if new and uncertain, direction for their lives. They could see the tragic events as "Walk This Way" signs. They could learn something about themselves from the experiences. These are the crises that create the opportunities; it takes crisis to open us to fundamental change.

Instead, many of us continue to struggle, allowing the struggle to drag us to our knees. We try to control our universe, never realizing that it cannot be controlled. We do not realize that we need to *let go* of control, to learn from these events and bend with the circumstances, and live closer to what is happening to us. Caught up in the substance of our lives, we miss the all-important process. We allow the events themselves to prevent us from seeing why they are happening to us.

Please understand that none of this is intended to diminish the seriousness or sadness of these major events. When "bad" things happen to us, we need to feel all of the emotions that go along with those things. We see stories on the news that bring tears to our eyes. Being without money, being without a job is indeed tragic and deeply saddening, but there are other ways of seeing the same incidents. If we accept them, these new points of view may help us see the same events in different lights that better enable us to work our way out of them. And since none of us knows "the truth," we have the chance to make up a version of reality that will make us feel a bit better and give us a new vantage point.

Our lives are not about the actual things that happen to us, though the events are no doubt important. They bring us joy or sadness or grief. Our lives are about the *process*, the "why" of things, and the opportunities these events bring us to learn, to evolve. We can never learn, we can never evolve, if we do not open ourselves up to change. By restricting ourselves, doing over and over again what has failed us in the past, we do not grow but only vegetate. It is in the process that the Tao, that God, speaks to us.

The Tao stands for achieving that which is sought through cooperation and not confrontation with the natural forces. One way we can let go of our need to control others is, paradoxically, by being out of control of ourselves and by trusting in the cycles, in the chaos. Such is the nature of the Tao, that apparent disasters can lead to their opposites and perhaps to harmony. I say "perhaps" because it is up to us to open ourselves to those possibilities, instead of fighting and resisting. It is the *yin* and the *yang*; the extreme of any situation may bring on the occurrence of its opposite, leading to harmonious change. When things get out of control, or seem that way to us, they are merely trying to right themselves, to find a balance and a harmony that is appropriate for the situation. If we are secure enough within ourselves to let this process occur, we may find balance for ourselves and then be able to allow it to others.

Such cycles may be very long term, however, and beyond our own small vision. Fearing the uncertainty of chaos, we want things to resolve themselves immediately. If we could see the connections that each event in our lives has with everything that came before, we might see how everything fits and could feel less uncomfortable with what seems to be chaos. Instead, we try to control the outside world, thinking somehow that this will make us secure. We resist change.

> Trusting the cycles, which is the same as trusting in the universe, in God, requires a very different perspective about ourselves. This trust allows us to accept differing views and alternative solutions that may seem odd or frighteningly new.[1]

It seems innate, however, that we change and let go of control only when crises in our lives demand it of us. As long as we are able to tolerate even the most unpleasant of conditions, as long as we think we have it under control, evidence to the contrary notwithstanding, we continue to fight and kick and scream against change. It is only when change forces itself upon us that we can find it "within our power" to let go and let change take its course.

This applies not only inside of ourselves but in the outer world as well. The reason for the revolutionary economic and social changes taking place in the former Soviet Union and in Eastern Europe is that those people have lived with profound pain for decades. Years of repression and economic deprivation finally became so excruciating that the sufferers were willing to risk the uncertainty of anything else. The barriers of resistance were broken because of the extent and depth of the crisis. There was little in their society which could shelter them from the harshness of the pain.

In the West, however, at least for the moment, we do not have the level of suffering that existed for the Soviets. We have many more buffers in our system which shield us for now from the extremes of crises. To avoid seeing homelessness and crime on television, we can change the channel with our remote control (an appropriate term) from the comfort of our easy chair. When we cannot flip enough channels to ease the pain of what we see, we go to a movie. If we are oppressed by our day at work, we can jump into the whirlpool bath or get into our fancy car and try to drive away from our problems. The people in the world who are truly suffering do not have those options. They are living at the extremes of life.

But our world is changing rapidly and, for many of us, it already is at a crisis stage. People who never knew unemployment are now without work. Entire job categories are being rendered obsolete by new technology. Change is needed for all of us, but until we reach a place of enough desperation for enough people that we are willing and able to change *en masse*, we collectively remain mired in our rigidity.

We refuse to open ourselves up to radically new ideas about the great social problems we face today. We would rather proceed, if at all, by increments, by inches. Instead of cutting military spending completely, we pretend that we are doing something by cutting it five percent. Instead of radically reforming our political system to attract creative individuals and new ideas about money and other issues, we decry our sorry state and complain about how our politicians lack vision. Instead of seeing social and economic disruption as the process of natural forces breaking out of the constrictions we have placed upon them and learning to go along with these trends, we seek fixes, quick and otherwise, by passing new laws, applying yet more restrictions, and thinking that we will be able to thereby control that which is out of our control. We do all of this out of fear of change, out of fear that we may have been wrong for all our lives. These are simply the external ways we show our internal fears.

We are afraid to try new concepts, about money and other issues, because we are afraid that if they do not work, we will have "failed." In Taoism, there is no failure—only opportunities to grow and learn. There are no mistakes, only openings. Everything that we have ever done or learned matters. (Although, so far, it is by no means clear where geometry fits in.) The concept of failure arises only when we have created expectations, human expectations, of how a particular set of circumstances should develop. If they vary from our expectations, we think we have failed. Letting go of these expectations, which is the same as letting go of our attempts to control our world, leads us to trust that whatever the outcome, it is simply part of the growth process. We are all growing, individually and, as a planet, together.

At the highest level, the insecurities felt by our government leaders cause them to turn their fear outward and project it toward some ill-defined enemy. It used to be the Soviet Union. Now it is Japan, or Iraq, or Libya, or whomever. It may be people of another race or another country. It may be the elderly, whose Social Security or Medicare funds, we are told, must be cut so that we may survive in the face of "the enemy" or so that we may reduce the nation's deficit.

Our leaders know how to talk about fear without calling it fear. They know how to talk about insecurity without calling it insecurity. And we, because of our own personal microstruggles, relate to the larger struggle and empathize with it, because it seems to give us some comfort from what we struggle with every day.

We Can Change All This

Many of us think it is easier, much easier, to merely let others take responsibility for our lives. We seem to have a stake in the perpetuation of our misery, suffering, and fear, as though that pain is the reality, and without it, we would be without self-definition. We feel we must continue to prove that we are as unworthy as our image of ourselves. As a result, we continue to carry our personal baggage each day into new situations, with new people, instead of realizing that it is stupid and that we can be free simply by being free. There is no value in this sort of self-fulfilling prophecy other than that it is self-fulfilling (at least we end up being right). Being a victim does not create freedom, however; rather, the opposite is true.

The Tao can help us let go, if only a bit, of that to which we cling. It allows us to believe that we are safe if we ease up just a little. The Tao can show us that there is no "out there" to take anything away from us. We are the "out there." Recognizing that the enemy is ourselves can give us a feeling of unity with all things and take away the fear. In the process, it can give us peace. As we grow more comfortable with the idea that there is nothing to control, we can become less fearful. Our security, we learn, comes from being secure within ourselves and not from something outside of ourselves. We begin to take responsibility for our own lives and conduct instead of searching for others to blame or fear.

Until then, the more difficult things become, the more we seek to control them. In the outer world, the more stagnant our economy becomes, for example, the more the cry is heard to restrict imports, erect barriers to free trade, take away social benefits from less-powerful groups such as students, welfare recipients, and those living in the inner cities. As it happens in our personal lives, the more restrictive we as a nation become, the worse the problems become, because other nations who are suffering because of our restrictive policies simply do the same as we are doing, and so everyone suffers even more. The more we restrict others, the more they rebel in their own ways. We end up with civil disorder, higher health care costs, and less-successful businesses hiring less-educated employees.

Letting go of control is the most difficult thing we will ever do. It is what life is all about. For those who whine, "It's t-o-o-o-o h-a-a-a-r-d!" we reply that the people of the former Soviet Union and in Eastern Europe, with no free press or right to assemble, with repression from every quarter, with secret police monitoring everyone, accomplished the single most wonderful and dramatic revolution in the history of humankind.

True Freedom

As long as we blame our predicaments on something outside of ourselves, we can never be free, because we must continue to exert all of our efforts toward controlling that outside force. Freedom, true freedom, is scary stuff indeed. It is illusive and transitory, and its manifestations and permutations are sometimes difficult to see. The hold of our past upon us is very strong; even the most free sometimes find themselves falling into self-made traps.

We frequently blame our predicament on our political leaders. In truth, however, our condition results not from the choices made by our leaders, but rather from the leaders we have chosen. Our leaders, who run our countries and determine how we spend our public money, got to their place as a result of our contributions, both of commission as well as omission. Those contributions have depended, in large part, on our view of the world, and that view has been determined, in large part, by our self-image. We vote our consciences, whether we realize it or not. We vote for those who reflect what we believe to be true. And as long as our views remain stagnant and stale, our leadership will mirror those views.

Freedom and integrity are inextricably intertwined. Integrity means sound and complete, as well as having principle, character, self-respect, wholeness, and unity. Freedom means independence in choice of conduct, as well as openness and emancipation. We cannot be truly free unless we are integrated. If our choices of action are governed by an outside force, real or imagined, which we feel exerts control over us, then we cannot, in any meaningful sense of the words, be free or act with integrity. We are not complete when our lives are determined by something external to ourselves.

To act with integrity means that we are free and complete. It allows for total boundlessness of choice. It allows for openness of action, unconstrained by the dictates of another. It allows true desires, as opposed to needs, to govern our lives. In short, it allows us to reach inside and find our true selves and act upon them. And once we find ourselves, we can then, and indeed only then, give to others, for we no longer have any need to be in fear of them. We no longer need worry that they will somehow take our selves and our security, because we know that security comes from inside, not from outside. Freedom comes not from having things, not from proclamations written on a piece of parchment, but from a deep sense of integration, of knowing that we are complete within ourselves. It is only then that freedom and integrity can be said to exist.

If we operate out of fear when it comes to money, by working in a job we hate because we are afraid of finding our calling, or on a larger level, by not allowing free immigration of people seeking to improve their own economic situations, our fear deprives us of our freedom and our integrity, for we must always be on guard against that which we fear. When we are able to connect with the natural order of things by feeling it inside our hearts, when we are able to trust enough in ourselves, in God, in the universe to let go of our attempts at controlling everything and everyone, only then can we be free. Taoist philosophy is about learning to let go. But letting go of the economic crutches we have created, of illusions about being victims of outside forces, would mean letting go of the excuses we have created for ourselves, and that is not easy.

Our individual and national reactions to the world do not give us the sense that we are truly free.

We are as much enslaved as African Americans or women were decades ago (and to a large degree still are). We proclaim ourselves to be free, though for 45 years we were dependent for much of our national definition on the then Soviet Union. Today we seem to be as dependent upon Japan for that definition. We are told that we and our economy are suffering because of Japanese products—"trade imbalance" it is called. We are unable to make choices free of these and other constraints. How we spend our money to help the poor, the un- and undereducated, the elderly; what we do for the people within our geographic borders; whether we fix the giant, sedan-eating potholes in our city streets—all this is conditioned upon how much money we have left after we protect ourselves from the current "significant other" that controls our actions. Additionally, we continue to pay high taxes because we continue to support a huge international military complex, and continue to run substantial budget deficits largely created by that same military mentality. We are victims of our perceived enemies much as some of us feel ourselves as victims of "the other" in our personal relationships.

There are those who are afraid of diversity because they see it as a threat. They search for answers that are clear and immutable and, when faced with the vagaries of the world, regress to old ideas or no ideas.

Unable to deal with multiplicity of choices, they see the world in either/or, black-and-white, zero-sum terms. Instead of viewing the world in this simplistic fashion, which can only lead to conflict because the choices are "with me or agin me," we can follow Taoist teachings that the world is full of many variations, many possibilities. But when we act out of a need to control ourselves and others, we are unable to see and act with this freedom of choice.

We have a need for uniformity in thought. Although we contend that we seek self-determination for the Other, it is not so. The only form of independence we will tolerate is one that makes the Other dependent upon us. We enslave, sometimes in subtle but still effective ways, such as through economic policies, those whose ideas differ from what we deem to be right. If we are in a position of power to make that determination, then our might becomes what is right. We are intolerant of the new because it is new.

We constantly retrench and argue the same arguments, which no longer have any meaning. We react to buzzwords that represent phrases or ideas, which enables us to think that we are thinking. In truth, however, this completely prevents thinking. Our thoughts become nothing but knee-jerk, Pavlovian responses to verbal stimuli. Words such as *communism*, *democracy*, *freedom*, and yes, *Taoism*, evoke this sort of response.

Even the term *America* is now a buzzword, for it no longer means what we believe it means. We are not secure enough within ourselves to question these buzzwords, for we have built our society upon them, and to question them would expose their fallacies and, in the process, our own. If, however, we can trust enough in ourselves to try the truly new, letting go of our original concepts of "truth," we may find solutions to our personal problems as well as those we face as humanity.

How Control Looks in the Outer World

Letting things simply be, allowing events to find their own level, is just the opposite of attempting to control them. All things, all events can, if left alone, find their level of balance and harmony, through the operation of the *yin* and *yang*. It is so in the natural world, and it is so in the world of money.

The Taoist concept of *yin* and *yang* explains the classic examples of freedom in the economic marketplace and the operation of supply and demand. When something reaches one extreme, the natural processes of harmony and balance can operate to bring about its opposite; and as the opposite reaches its extreme, it then can cause its opposite to take over. It is not a static phenomenon, but one that is in a constant state of movement. While each component is always changing, it is changing in relationship to all other components. But there must be freedom of all such forces if the natural processes are to find balance and harmony.

Under *yin* and *yang*, as one company, one nation, gains significant control over a market (supply), that company or nation generally raises prices and decreases services to maximize profits, and does so as long as people are willing to pay the price (demand). As prices rise and services diminish, another company or nation enters the marketplace and provides the same services at lower prices, siphoning off the market share of the original company or nation. This is the natural process. Nature abhors a vacuum, it has been said. As other companies and nations follow, capitalizing on this demand, and as the supply of goods or services increases, prices drop to meet the demand; then the balance point, the harmony, the equilibrium is reached. That particular market is acting according to the laws of nature, not the laws of man. There is no need for trade and other restrictions in such a market.

We have in place, however, restrictive economic policies that keep these natural forces from working. People throughout the world, including those in this country, are starving—even while we pay farmers, with our tax money, not to farm, and buy up surplus food or give subsidies in order to artificially maintain prices at certain levels to benefit the farmers. And yet as a result, we all pay higher prices at the grocery store. Without such artificial restraints, prices for surplus commodities could fall. If they fell far enough, some farmers might stop planting those crops and the supply might then diminish, thereby raising prices. If they rose high enough, new suppliers could enter the market to take advantage of those higher prices, and the cycle could continue, always in balance. Low prices might also mean that poorer nations could then afford to purchase U.S. commodities to feed their starving and save lives. Without artificial supports, prices could be free to find an equilibrium.

We restrict imports of certain goods and thereby create an artificial market for domestic goods of the same type. Domestic producers no longer have the pressure of the natural forces of competition, and so domestic goods tend to rise in price even as quality suffers. A few make money at the expense of everyone. Restricting the imports of any goods means prices for the same goods produced here will rise due to lessening of competition. The "voluntary" restraints imposed on Japanese car makers, for example, reduce competition and raise the prices—for Japanese cars and domestic cars, as well.

The deregulation of the airline industry in the 1980s brought about major fare reductions when competition over routes increased. As prices fell, certain companies went out of business or were acquired by other companies. As the number of companies got smaller and competition was thus reduced, prices again began to rise. The demand not only remained the same but in many instances increased, and new airlines stepped in to fill the supply gap, thereby lowering prices again and providing additional services. Society as a whole benefited from greater choice, more leg room, and lower prices. (And marginally better food. Those tiny eating utensils remain the same, however.)

Another example is the deregulation of the telephone industry, long a controlled monopoly. In 1984, when the monopoly was ended, competition appeared in the form of numerous alternative long-distance carriers, and the cost of long-distance services decreased. Even today, with satellites, cellular service, and microwaves replacing land lines, competition exists even at the local level.

But perhaps the most significant evidence of the power of nature and balance to win over regulation comes from the example of oil. When OPEC was formed and the cartel regulated supply, prices went up. How well most of us remember the news-making price of $1.00 per gallon! Over a relatively short period of time, however, demand began to decrease; the world began to buy gasoline-efficient automobiles, mostly from Japan, and we started to develop other conservation measures. Alternative fuels were being researched. Arguments within OPEC over supply (production), along with continued reduced demand, further demonstrated the power of the marketplace over the forces of regulation. Although prices stabilized after initially rising dramatically, we eventually got used to higher prices for gasoline; we returned to our demand for more powerful and hence less gas-efficient automobiles, thereby again raising prices and leading inevitably to Gulf War I. I say "unfortunately" only from the consumer point of view; from the Taoist point of view, it is all part of the same ebb and flow.

The underlying truth here is that left alone, all things can find balance in relationship to everything else.

> The principle is that if everything is allowed to go its own way the harmony of the universe will be established, since every process in the world can "do its own thing" only in relation to all others.[2]

In our personal lives, we live with much economic restriction and repression. We live beyond our means, in debt, exacerbating this debt by excessive spending.

As I have explained, this can lead to the view that controlling our world is appropriate behavior; in turn, that can lead to believing that we should have real-world restrictions.

War is chief among the forces of control, economic regulation, and repression. We, in the form of our government, take vast amounts of money—$1.6 trillion during the last ten years, growing by nearly $300 billion each year—out of the natural market and invest it in arms, which have no broad-based market at all and which might not exist at all without government interference. The natural market benefits society at large and depends only on unrestricted demand. It is the market for goods and services that benefit people in general, society as a whole. Most of us have no demand for missiles but do want home electronics and shoes and sugar. Arms have little in the way of multiple productivity, in that their production employs relatively few workers, most of them highly skilled. The end product, a tank, submarine, or the like, is a finite product, generating no further jobs or spending. But build a house instead of a missile, and the lumber industry gets jobs, the plumbing industry gets jobs, the electronic appliance industry gets jobs, and gardeners and painters and cable TV people get jobs. The evidence is overwhelming that investment in civilian forms of productivity—housing, cars, schools, roads and bridges, and so on

—produces infinitely larger numbers of jobs than does investment in the military.

From a Taoist viewpoint, military spending is based upon fear and separateness, whereas investment in civilian ventures is based upon hope and unity. (More on war coming up.) We must be willing to open our minds to widely differing ideas, ideas that make us uncomfortable because of their newness. Like war, money must be considered in a moral, ethical, and indeed, spiritual context—not just from an objective, impersonal point of view.

A Role for Government

We cannot be limited in our thinking to either/or, that is, to either free markets or regulation. Taoism speaks of less government, less taxes, less interference, but in some circumstances it is necessary to interfere with markets when there are no operative competitive forces that can act to stabilize and balance those markets. Certain industries do not have competition, for example. Until people in those industries understand that price gouging and exorbitant profits are unnatural, it may be necessary to interfere in those markets so that people are not hurt. There are other situations requiring some level of interference in order to maintain harmony. This is the "heart" factor.

The masters advocate a pluralistic yet egalitarian society with minimal government interference and maximum opportunity for individual fulfillment. They also propose a conscious balance between the human and natural worlds, regarding it as so necessary that they refer to this balance itself as divine.[3]

Balance is the operative word here. Balance means, in economic terms, that the ism must give way to what works. This applies whether the ism is capitalism, socialism, or Taoism.

Taoist ideology tells us that we should therefore be free enough to include any idea that works under the circumstance. Our choices are limitless once we unshackle ourselves from the constraints of an ism. We limit ourselves when we think only in terms of our own benefits, of what is good only for us. Thus we develop the either/or mentality, because what is good for us may be bad for another, who responds accordingly. We are then at odds and, sometimes, at war. The concepts of "good" and "bad" do not make sense. They block us from thinking more creatively about solutions.

It should be fairly clear that unbridled freedom in economics can and indeed has lead to significant abuse of the system, through greed, unethical practices, and the like. Until human nature progresses to the point where the good of one is perceived as the good of all, there will always be those who need some sort of government assistance to keep them from being so abused. Therefore, letting go of economic controls must be accompanied by the heart factor, by love.

Too many of us would leave the poor, the uneducated, and the elderly to fend for themselves, because it offends our particular ism—in this instance, free-market capitalism. Compassion loses out. The heart gives way to the intellect. Rationality overwhelms faith. Even as we debate how to reduce budget deficits, we are already targeting these groups for cuts in aid.

It is our job, in the role of government, to protect those groups and individuals and to allow the Taoist principles to operate within a minimal set of government regulations. During these present and coming times of great reformation, it is the obligation of government, of us, to spend our money making the transitions as easy as can be. Those whose jobs are displaced by massive military spending cutbacks or whose industries are eliminated due to competition must be retrained and given monetary support, to keep them from hunger and homelessness. During this time, we should be spending our money on assisting those without educational skills to acquire the skills necessary to make them competitive in the fields of new technology. But we are not doing so, although we talk as though we are.

When it comes to finding a balance between leaving markets free and taking care of the poor, the uneducated, the welfare-based groups in our society, it is the role of government not to put these groups into servitude forever but to assist them, over time, in becoming self-sufficient—through training, economic assistance, and education. What is important here is for this form of government interference to be temporary, although "temporary," in the context of human development, may involve assistance for some time. The purpose of such involvement is to create fully independent and self-empowered persons over the long haul, so that they can live fully functioning lives without need of paternalistic protectionism.

To achieve balance and harmony, each of us owes it to ourselves, to our children, to others, to maximize our own potential and skills. In the end, we are each responsible for our own fates; no government will be there to live our lives for us. It is up to all of us to take charge of our own lives and not live like victims. And so the *yin* to the *yang* of government interference is the decision made by each of the recipients of such assistance to become free of the need for that assistance. The choice is up to each of us.

Today, however, our society shuns those who need assistance. We pretend to care, but when it comes to spending money on programs to help these groups, our priorities break down. We are cynical and hypocritical. Our government leaders, whom we elect, know that knowledge is power and, theoretically, is available to everyone. Those who obtain knowledge might gain power that they today lack. Thus, while proclaiming its desire to provide educational opportunities for minorities, government may in fact fear the gains those groups might realize as a result of acquiring knowledge.

Traditional calls from our leaders for "workfare," where those who seek public assistance must work for it, are hollow indeed—hollow because these same leaders never infuse the welfare system with enough money to make workfare work. When it fails, they can say, "See, I told you so. These people just don't want to improve themselves." This type of program is always the first to feel the scalpel of budget cuts. These programs are seldom combined with other help programs, such as self-image counseling, teenage pregnancy prevention, or incentives to create jobs in minority areas so that there are places to work. Current examples of workfare programs are designed to fail. They are designed to fail because they are perceived as being for the limited benefit of the Other and not for Us. We do not see how empowering everyone will empower the society and all of us in it.

City and state governments throughout the nation are facing difficult economic times, and this has lead to our having to choose sides. Do we want education or welfare? We cannot have both, we are told. We have limited ourselves to only two choices because our thinking is such that we believe economic resources are scarce, and in our zero-sum world, if we give to Them, We will have less. Of course, the fact that we have deprived ourselves of the vast amounts of money spent on war makes our view of scarcity a very real reality. We refuse to pay more taxes to fund schools, but protest loudly when teachers' salaries are cut. We complain loudly about lack of adequate health care for many in our nation, yet selfishness and greed and narrow-mindedness keep us from modifying our system to help even ourselves.

Internationally, the industrialized nations give only a small percentage of their revenues to priority human needs such as education, rural water supplies, and family planning. We see only infinitesimal amounts of money devoted to improving the human condition throughout the world, although improving that condition would go a long way toward ending the underlying causes of war, and so we can see that things are way out of balance.

Government's role is also to act as a stimulus when the economy is dragging, not simply by inter-fering with interest rates that benefit one segment of the economy over another, but by becoming a con-sumer of goods and services. During the Great

Depression, the government put thousands of people to work building bridges and buildings, repairing roads, and so on. Similarly, during today's economic transition, it is the responsibility of government to employ teachers, fund research into alternative fuels, and support other such projects that will serve as the needed stimulus. Money for these jobs would be readily available if liberated from our war-making budget. But due to ideological constraints, we have refused to make government funds available for such purposes, although we have no difficulty in providing money for war production. On the same day as the announcement that the Air Force had awarded a major contract for the then Strategic Defense Initiative ("Star Wars"), a major car manufacturer announced it was cutting back on developing electric vehicles because the market had not yet developed enough to support production.

In sum, there is more than enough money available to fund all sorts of socially valuable programs— once we stop spending our money on war. But war is representative of our need for personal, internal attempts at controlling our outer world, in fear of being out of control, resulting in economic and social policies that are the concrete attempts at controlling that which we fear.

Principle 3:
Learn to See the Connections

The connection between our personal views about money and other issues, and how we see our world, seems clear. Each event that occurs in the universe, in our individual lives, is part of an orderly progression of events. Each subsequent event is a necessary consequence from the prior event and is, in turn, the cause of the next event. Our lives are harmonious wholes. We are connected to everything that has gone before, and everything that comes after will be in part the result of who we are today and how we behave. If we had a long enough point of view, we would be able to see these connections.

This does not mean that we are predestined to follow any particular course. Rather, it means the universe, God, offers us certain possibilities in the form of the things that happen to us, and we have the choice to see those possibilities as opportunities to learn. If we find connections among the events of our lives, we may then be able to see how they have given us opportunities, and we may learn how to look at ourselves in the future. I suggest this same concept applies to outer world events, as well.

This point of view may help us see why things occur when they do. If we go back far enough into the connections, we may be able to see their real causes and then look for creative solutions to our problems.

For example, if we believe in emotional scarcity, that is probably how we see the world at large. There is not enough emotional abundance in our personal lives to feed us. We may not have had enough love when we were children, and so we believe there is not enough raw material, oil, coal, whatever, to go around. Therefore, just as we need to control our personal world to keep from losing what we believe we will lose should we let go, as though it were coming from the outside, so, too, do we need to control other people and nations, through war, indebtedness, and repression, lest they rise up and take whatever stuff we think they will take.

> This economy of emotional scarcity, which is the source of so much jealousy and conflict and resentment, is really a myth. It's a kind of mag-

ical thinking, which vastly exaggerates our impact on the rest of the world. It's not like that at all. What you achieve doesn't take anything away from anyone else.[1]

We look for real-world events to tell us that our personal-world view is right. And when we act in accordance with that view, we generally turn out to *be* right. We create the very enemies we fear, just so that we can be right.

If we believe strongly that scarcity abounds, then we will probably be resistant to change, in our personal lives as well as in the world in general, because we will believe that change will lead to disaster. If we have the mindset of poverty that scarcity breeds, then we will fear anyone and anything that we believe threatens our security, including immigrants to our land, changes in the way we live our lives, and so on. The teachings of the Tao—that there is no scarcity because the universe is an integrated whole—will be lost on us.

The Tao teaches that nothing occurring in the world happens in a vacuum. Everything is related to everything else, and we, by our own conduct, by the way we think, create the world. Let me give an example of these connections, to tie into the discussion of our personal economic viewpoints.

Few of us think each time we go to the automated teller machine at the bank that we are participating in the perpetuation of governmental policies, both economic as well as social. There is a connection nonetheless. We deposit our money in the bank, and the bank lends much of it out and invests other portions of it. Examine the financial statement from your bank and you will probably see, generally as the bank's largest asset, government securities. Our banks, and individuals throughout the world, purchase Treasury bills, bonds, and notes (all government IOUs), because they are believed to be very secure. When I spoke earlier of our national debt, I was referring to these government securities, which are sold to finance that debt. The savings bond you received for graduation or some other event was a debt instrument.

Our government takes the money it raises by selling these bills, bonds, and notes and uses it, as tax money is used, to finance programs.

There are, of course, many commendable things that governments do—but there is much that is antisocial as well. Funding the huge military budget, giving grants and loans to nations who repress their people, to nations who use that money to buy military weapons, often from us, are some examples of antisocial expenditures. And, as we shall discuss later, part of government revenues go toward the U.S. contribution to the International Monetary Fund and the World Bank, some of whose policies result in oppression for the poorest peoples of the world.

So it is not only our tax money that connects us to the system, but our checking and savings accounts as well. Although there may be nothing we can effectively do to live without using such accounts, we can at least understand that all of us are part of "the system," giving us all the more reason to become aware of how our government's economic programs, which are using our money, are implemented.

Furthermore, any discussion of economic and social problems must involve a discussion of causes. Where most such discussions fall short is that the "causes" discussed are not, in fact, the causes at all, but merely the symptoms of an underlying issue that never gets discussed. We end up arguing and fighting about the last argument, which was nothing more than an argument and a war about the previous argument before that. We believe that the last argument justifies the present argument, that the last "Oh! Yeah?!" justifies the present retaliation, but the bottom line is that it is all made-up stuff. Most people are unwilling, or unable, to go back far enough into a given issue to see that war, for example, might have been avoided had the roots been unveiled for what they were.

We can look at events on the global scale as we look at events in our personal lives. If we learn to release our fear of the uncertainty of the new and begin to see where we truly are and how we got here, we may begin to see the connections. Doing this may enable us to avoid similar consequences in the future: These are the connections of our collective lives.

Consider, for example, Henry VIII. Because he could not persuade the Pope to let him divorce a barren queen over 400 years ago, people today are being killed in Northern Ireland. King Henry decided to set up his own church, the Protestant Anglican Church, and then he decided to impose that new church on all the people he controlled. When the Catholics in what became Northern Ireland resisted, the troubles began, and the origin of the Irish Republican Army was born, although no one knew it at the time.

Because Karl Marx, a not-very-successful German writer living in England over 150 years ago, put together a theory about a different social and economic order to deal with the working-class conditions of the day, for nearly 50 years the world faced the threat of nuclear annihilation. Today we are still coping with the proliferation of those weapons, which resulted directly from the ideological conflict between the United States and the Soviet Union, and we have some of the most polluted and toxic sites in the world in weapons manufacturing plants. Because of Marx's theory, tens of thousands of people were killed in places like Vietnam, Korea, El Salvador, Nicaragua, and Hungary, and many talented screenwriters and actors could get no work in Hollywood in the 1950s — some of them killed themselves, leaving their families devastated.

Because the Spanish conquistadors centuries ago were given grants of land in the New World as rewards for their discoveries and shipment to the Mother Country of such vital products as indigo and bananas, the peasants of Central America were brutally destroyed, both physically and economically, in the name of democracy, by the successors to those landed wealthy.

It's like burned toast. When two people in any relationship sense that there is something wrong but are unable to come to an understanding about the true nature of their feelings, they argue about symptoms. She is unhappy about herself. He is worried about his masculinity or about the meaning of his life. So they argue about money or, more likely, the lack of it. Neither one can or will deal with these basic problems, so they argue about who burned the toast. They argue about previous arguments.

On a grander scale, it's like international burned toast. The historical roots of the world's pressing issues have been lost in the overlay of symptoms brought by the intervening years. Today we no longer talk about the roots of the issues, for if we did, the present struggles and destruction would seem silly indeed and would pull out from under us the rug upon which we base our existence. We would, in short, have to rethink the way we look at the whole world. Such fundamental changes do not come easily.

Everything leads to everything else; there are no events of any consequence that do not lead to other events and other consequences. When we create a situation fraught with danger, we have set into motion a chain of events that we may be unable later to control except at a great price.

At the heart of all change on a large scale is change on the very personal scale. Unless all of us see ourselves as connected to everyone else, we will continue to have the attitude of separateness that has created not only war, but economic dislocation. In the monetary arena, change in the outer world will occur when we as individuals become the kind of businesspeople who see ourselves connected to the entirety of the universe, so that abuse of some persons, and excessive greed and profits, which serve in the end to be our undoing, are no longer the operative mindset. We are not separate individuals when we go to work but rather should employ the same values that we have when we are at home. The process of growth, which is what we are all about, can lead to a new kind of business ethic, and this can lead in turn to less need for restrictions on the universe.

This growth depends on developing a sense of how our individual conduct may affect others. As said previously, it depends upon understanding the wider context in which we live and work. Included within this concept is the entire notion of how we measure value and worth; economic indices in general must be changed to reflect our relationship to the entire planet and the interconnectedness of all things.

At present, economists measure only things that can be given numerical amounts. This has its shortfalls: It cannot tell us the true social costs of anything. For example, the gross domestic product and other such indices do not measure the quality of goods and services and so cannot tell us whether our product is good or bad for the society. It cannot tell us about the quality of our lives or whether the air we breathe and the water we drink are killing us. It does not tell us the social impact of unemployment on the unemployed or on their children. How many adults today, children or grandchildren of the Great Depression, are still living with that stigma, which now takes the form of over-work, drug abuse, child abuse, heart disease, cancer, and so on?

Because we are unable to measure certain true, if hidden, costs, we pretend they do not exist. How can we quantify the cost of pollution when we cannot measure the loss of pleasure and other nonmonetary benefits from acid rain and what it does to wildlife and streams and rivers? What is the true cost of toxic spill cleanups when we cannot measure the destroyed peace of mind of those who drink the water from the river just contaminated, after the local government agency tells them it is safe? Down deep, we all know that the water may not be as safe as we have been told, so each time our child catches a sniffle, do we fear some catastrophic illness? How is that fear to be mea-sured? What is the effect of war on our children when the war is solely for the purpose of making the world safe for oil production? That these factors cannot be measured does not make them less real.

We seem to be willing to accept at face value certain statistical information provided by economists, pri-marily because most of us lack knowledge sufficient to rebut the numbers. But sometimes the costs of our own living are sufficient to make us question, if we are of a mind to do so. For example, at the end of each year the

U.S. Department of Commerce announces that the consumer price index, which is the measure of retail inflation for all of us consumers, has risen x% for the year. As a result, the cost-of-living adjustment for people receiving Social Security, people receiving welfare payments and such, is increased by that percentage, to cover the stated increase in the "cost of living."

But often, the determinants used by the statisticians bear little relationship to what actually takes place in the market. As a result, we may find that prices for certain foods and other items that we actually use may have increased far beyond that stated increase in the cost of living. What this suggests is that whatever information is used by the statisticians may not be related to reality. Perhaps it also means that the figures are intentionally kept low by using such irrelevant information because it enables government to keep its payments to such groups as low as possible, leaving greater amounts of money to be spent on items for more powerful groups, such as megabusinesses and the military. In effect, we may be really talking about nonsense, because these numbers may belie the true circumstances in which many of us find ourselves.

Another example: Economists, wanting to measure "consumer confidence" in the economic state of our country, use as one measure the amount of personal debt we incur. The thinking is that the more debt we accumulate, the greater our confidence must be in our economic prospects, because it shows that we anticipate having jobs and the ability to pay off the debt. I suppose in some perverse sense this may be so, but such a statistic does not reveal the nonmonetary effects of such debt—such as loss of sleep in worry, or the huge social effects such debt may have if we guess wrong and are unable to pay it off.

Money and economics are taught as a separate and distinct discipline from sociology and urban studies. We tend to deal with numbers, almost in the abstract, rather than allowing any input as to how these numbers affect those whom they define. Incorporated into what economic theories we do now have must be social and political realities.

Another example: During certain economic times called "full production," the existence of "full employment" (that is, a decrease in the unemployment rate, meaning that more people are working and supporting themselves and their families and building self-esteem) is seen by some theorists as a "bad" statistic—because greater employment can lead to inflation. The idea behind the theory is, apparently, that if more people are working, there will be greater demands for labor, thereby driving up wages, and more money in circulation, making greater demands on the available products and services, thereby driving up prices for those goods and services. A statistic that has deep personal meaning (as opposed, for example, to one which measures durable goods) is thus turned on its head by our current value systems.

We look at social problems in isolated categories, as though they were separate from everything else. We do not understand the concept of relationships so integral to Taoism. As a result, the way we talk and think about how "well" we are doing is not in keeping with the measure of how the planet as a whole is doing. For example, during a time when the United States had the highest level of poverty in nearly three decades, and the highest level of teenage pregnancies in 15 years, we decried those statistics even as we failed to see their connection to rising welfare claims, skyrocketing health insurance costs even for those who could pay for it, more high-school dropouts, diminished funding for education, and the entire country's reduced competitiveness.

In 1992, Los Angeles's house collapsed from within—even though, on the surface, all was fine (save for the smog, the traffic, the homelessness, the high unemployment, the barriers between rich and poor, the high crime rate, the drug problem, the declining availability of health care, the school dropout rate, and the lack of adequate funding for public education). It helps to ignore this stuff when the sun shines.

What we saw in the violence and looting that came to the surface in Los Angeles shows just how close to chaos we all are living. We saw how even the slightest push would cause our house of cards to crumble in front of our eyes. Not only did we fail to anticipate the trouble before it began, we pretended it was over when it seemed to be over. The first day after the citywide dusk-to-dawn curfew was lifted, the Dow Jones Industrial Average rose 42.04 points, to close at a then record high level. Business went on as usual, even as the implications of the rioting failed to sink in. The urban riots of the 1960s were a faded and distant memory, but the symptoms remain despite our attempts to ignore them. The events in Los Angeles were simply the latest symptom to surface. They represented the entirety of the world.

Another example: There is a school of thought about the recent free trade agreement between the United States and Mexico that environmental concerns should not be included within the agreement, at least at the beginning. It is thought that we should let Mexican business grow without care about the environment and then, after those businesses are established, we can insist on enforcement. Forgetting for the moment the expense and difficulty to retrofit industry with environmental controls, such as installing scrubbers on smokestacks to cut down acid emissions (which we are later told is too expensive, so we cannot do it), the argument presumes that economic growth is independent and separate and apart from the health of the people and the planet.

The very pesticides and other chemicals we have found too toxic to use in the United States (and have then shipped to other nations having less concern for that toxicity, such as Mexico) will now be appearing in the very food and other products we sought to protect. The environmental region between the U.S. and Mexico, which is the region most affected by this proposed agreement, has rivers that flow out of Mexico and into the United States. Toxics dumped into these rivers by American manufacturers attempting to save money end up in American drinking water. This region's air-flow patterns bring airborne pollution directly into Southern California, Texas, and Arizona. The wheel comes full circle, as it always does— because the planet is an integrated whole, and the totality of the air and water remains the same. There is no place else for this stuff to go.

This situation is yet another example of the Taoist and Buddhist concepts of *dualism*, of seeing a person as the controller of his or her world as opposed to being contained as only one integral part of it. This argument places economic satisfaction above all other concerns, as though if someone has a job, that makes life better. We see the fallacy of this argument when people with jobs are suffering enormous health risks, of cancer and other life-threatening diseases due to toxics contaminating the water and the air, toxics that come directly from the products the people manufacture at their jobs.

Dualism occurs in other forms. Recall the discussion about the old map of the world: By dividing the Earth into separate nations, each nation wanting to be self-sufficient from all others, we create the dualistic view. If, on the other hand, we viewed the planet as an integrated unit, then each area would be able to pursue what economists call its "comparative advantage"; that is, it could do what it does best, relying on the other parts of the planet to supply what it lacked. Such a view leads to the concept of abundance, not scarcity. There is only scarcity when lines separate us, because resources inevitably fall on one side of a line and not the other. Lines about money and resources lead only to war and to divisive thinking. When the lines are eliminated, there is no scarcity. There is enough for everyone.

It would skew the discussion to focus solely on American viewpoints. From Bangkok to Beijing, from Denpasar to Delhi, people are emitting toxic, killing pollutants trying to become industrial powerhouses by attracting western industry. To impose pollution controls on these businesses would make the respective countries less attractive for investment. In Indonesia, for example, one can hardly see the rice paddies because of the omnipresent haze and smoke that overhangs the cities. In Bangkok, a city with significant traffic congestion, the government continues to import thousands of cars to meet growing demand, few of which cars have pollution control devices.

The Asian example is important, for it shows the relevance of changes on a global scale. Given that Asia is one of the fastest growing parts of the world, and given that many Asian people live in cities, and given that these cities are great sources of pollution, it seems that whatever we in the western world do to control this toxicity is almost beside the point, since the Asian pollution may simply overwhelm our attempts at control.

More connections: Economist after economist tells us that the key to financial survival for all countries lies in increased international trade. From an economic standpoint, it is clear that if there is no one to whom we can sell our goods, our own production will fail. The result is significant job loss, leading to greater budget deficits as a consequence of falling tax revenues and increased social expenditures such as unemployment insurance and welfare. Accordingly, it is in our own best interest to support the economies of everyone else, so that we in turn can survive. The economic survival of one depends upon the economic survival of all.

But political leaders fail to take this reasoning to the next step, because they are ruled by fear and political concerns. When we act in our own interests to the exclusion of everyone else, as though only we are at the center of the world map, we destroy jobs, economies, and, indeed, lives in the other countries affected—not to mention the effects on Americans with jobs related to exporting. Latin American debt, for example, now totals hundreds of billions of dollars. This represents money borrowed throughout the 1970s and 1980s during times of inflation and vast oil revenues. When world economies cooled and oil prices fell in the middle to late 1980s, these Latin American nations found themselves unable to repay the loans. In order to qualify for new international loans from the World Bank and the International Monetary Fund, to be used in part to repay old loans, recipient countries are required to impose austerity measures to reduce public spending and conserve capital. Foreign governments are forced, as Mexico and the Dominican Republic and El Salvador have been forced, to raise prices on basic foodstuffs, cut back on programs to aid the poor, or devalue their currency to attract investment. Those who are hurt the most are the people with no flexibility in their economic situations. When these governments offer so little in the way of a future for their people, violence and revolution are often the result, since these same governments usually offer little means of peaceful redress. Literally overnight, the same poor who were on Day 1 the backbone of the nation, on Day 2 are instantly transformed into the dreaded "Communists" or "terrorists." That these poor are merely trying to feed their families is of course never acknowledged. Despite the recent fall of the chief Communist power, we have considered our world in dualistic terms for so long that many of our leaders fail to see the continued failing in this approach. And so the poor remain repressed by economic conditions, even while no active war is being fought. This is one way we control others by our economic policies.

It takes little imagination to see the parallels in our own country. We, too, are suffering under significant debt, and our poor, our uneducated, our elderly,

our ill are suffering as a result. We tolerate these conditions because we have developed the separation of
which I have spoken, which allows us to see other
groups as enemies. If They have, then We must lack.
We are no different from those we oppress; we just
have more diversions to keep us from seeing our sim-
ilarities.

And as we regress further economically from the
powerhouse nation we were in the 1950s and 1960s,
as we lose market share to other hitherto powerless
countries, as our economic problems and all their
attendant consequences become more apparent to us,
rather than rethinking our premises, we further
narrow our views. We look for enemies outside our
country to blame for our deterioration. We allow our
leaders to convince us that it is someone else's fault,
and if we conquer this or that enemy, we will get back
to where we were.

They tell us—indeed, we demand that they tell
us—that they are going to protect "American" jobs,
as though there really were such a thing today. Virtually everything today is made everywhere. Parts made
in one country are shipped to another for assembling.
Goods are transported by container ships made in one
nation and registered in another. "Japanese" cars are
made in Detroit, California, Cleveland, and Mexico.

"American" cars are made in Canada and Korea. Additionally, there are many "American" jobs that depend upon international markets. Where would all the salespeople be without these "foreign" cars manufactured in other nations? What about our garment industry, which depends heavily on the textile industries of other nations? One of the justifications offered for the war against Iraq was that it was about "jobs, jobs, jobs." But what *are* "American" jobs and "American" products? For that matter, what is "America"? Even if "America" is still in the center of the map, does that concept have meaning any longer? Is it time to rethink that concept, all our concepts?

Taoist Approaches

Having outlined some of the problems, we shall examine how Taoism helps us to think about them in new ways. The answer, of course, lies in finding what it means in the "real world" to go along with the natural processes of the universe, to use a problem's strength to defeat it. This involves learning to use the natural forces of the universe and not trying to dominate them. It is again a way of letting the problem solve itself, rather than making up a solution that involves unnatural forces, or in other words, "Submit to Nature if you would reach your goal."[2]

Accordingly, Taoism tells us that we must eliminate the poverty, hunger, malnutrition, corruption, and illiteracy that cause people to grasp at any alternative that puts food into the mouths of their children. We must provide agronomists, not soldiers; doctors, not mercenaries; food, not napalm; and teachers, not military advisors. We must engage in long-term, sustained approaches for bettering the conditions of those who would rebel, so that they have no reason to rebel. We must strive to make them as healthy and secure as we ourselves would like to be, for unless everyone is secure, no one is.

A number of years ago, when the Soviet Union was "the enemy," it proposed building a natural gas pipeline from Siberia to Western Europe. The United States was strongly opposed to the pipeline because, we were told, it would make Western Europe dependent upon the Soviets for gas. Exactly the point—but clearly the wrong conclusion. The more interdependent we are, Europe for gas and Russia for desperately needed western currency, the less the likelihood for war. Neither side wants to destroy the other, because doing so would be self-destruction. This is a concrete, real-world example of how to use the strength of the enemy (its gas) to defeat that enemy (communism), as well as a solution that uses the natural forces of self-interest to solve the problem. (This will be discussed again later.)

Nations are artifices of humanity—lines drawn on a map, the result of wars and conquests—and bear no relationship to nature. The economic interdependence about which we now hear so much demonstrates that national boundaries are irrelevant. Foreign interests now own significant portions of U.S. manufacturing capability. We are electronically intertwined via fax machines, computers, satellites, and digital money transfers. National boundaries are obsolete. At the turn of the twentieth century, there were only 60 nations in the world; today there are 190, and as revolutions and ethnic wars continue to occur, new lines will be drawn in place of old ones. We do not have to eliminate these nations in *fact* (thereby destroying the flag-making market); they can be eliminated in our *minds*, as vestiges of the past when it comes to thinking about money and self-interest.

It is only the rigid who hold onto the concept of separate nations. The Taoist concept of seeing the world as a unified whole must, if it is to be valid for this reformation, take real-world form. But for these examples to be accepted and adopted, we must be willing to let go of the old ideas that have dominated our thinking for eons.

> It'll be a better world when we quit being fools about some mildewed town or ten acres of swampland just because we happened to be born there.[3]

Principle 4:
Stop Pretending Ideas Work When They Do Not

There is a very old joke about a man who saw another man looking at the ground, at night, under a lamppost. The first man asked the second what he was doing, and the second man replied that he had lost his keys over there . . . in the alley. When asked why he was looking here, under the lamppost, if he'd lost his keys over there, in the alley, the second man replied that there was more light over here . . . under the lamppost.

You may remember, during the early days of the Clinton administration, that one of the President's nominees for Attorney General withdrew her nomination after she revealed that she had hired, as a nanny for her children, an "illegal" alien. There was much furor and public debate about whether the candidate should withdraw her name. It turned out that millions of Americans have done exactly the same thing, because in the market for nannies only women from lesser developed nations, such as Mexico, were applicants for those jobs.

We have substantial immigration laws and large, if easily avoided, fences to keep out persons from economically impoverished nations who attempt to come here to find work. We make exceptions, of course — not based on any logic or rationality, but rather on the power of the lobbying group seeking the exemption. So we allow Mexican "illegals" to harvest our agricultural products because the economic base for such goods would be destroyed if growers had to pay prevailing U.S. wages. But we do not allow these "illegals" to bus the dishes in restaurants or sew the seams in our clothing factories . . . or care for our children.

We have raised the "lines on a map" idea, learned as children in grade school, to a silly and irrational place. We spend millions of dollars a year "defending" our borders from "attack" by people from Mexico and Central America and China; this spending is not only ineffective, but the millions are then unavailable for the more creative and productive economic needs of our society. And we spend this money even though we fully acknowledge that it is useless and wasteful — because it makes us feel we are "doing something" about the "problem." It is a short-term response to a much deeper problem, one that requires us to examine our personal, national, and international economic policies and thoroughly revise them, so that the nations from which these job-seekers come may have their own economies substantially improved. Recall the earlier discussion about international lending policies, our own acceptance of debt as a way of living, our checking accounts, and so on. In every way, we are the reasons "illegals" are coming here in the first place.

But long-term solutions are difficult to sell to short-term thinkers, people who want easy, if wrong, answers. There is more light over here, where the short-term answers are, than over there, where the real solutions lie. And so we have not learned the lessons of "Nannygate."

Living in accord with the Tao in this context means doing what works, "going with the flow." Rather than committing ourselves to a particular ism and pursuing that ism to our destruction like lemmings to the sea, we should be flexible enough to examine a situation and decide how to handle it, free of the constraints we have placed on ourselves. It means making decisions based on a multiplicity of choices, rather than one choice dictated by a previously committed "buzzword" ideology. It means finding a solution that works virtually by itself, rather than through the force of border patrols.

To impose nationalistic concepts on economics by repressive immigration laws flies in the face of nature and confronts the laws of supply and demand that are natural in their effect. Open borders between the United States and Mexico (or Central America or China) mean that the attraction of jobs in this country could be filled by those whose standard of living makes working for lower wages possible. If we artificially impose a line on a map and restrict the natural flow of labor to the U.S., these jobs remain unfilled because the pay rate is too low to attract U.S. workers, forcing U.S. employers to hire "illegals." Additionally, because the lure of earning even a subsistence wage attracts immigrants despite the laws, the immigrants then become subject to extortion by greedy employers who threaten to deport workers who ask for more money or want to unionize. Some pay huge sums to be shipped here like cattle in overcrowded boats.

These circumstances develop because there are laws against immigration. If there were no restrictions on immigration, then the available jobs could be filled by the larger pool of workers, until that supply matched the demand. If the demand for labor continued to increase as the supply remained constant, the salaries offered might increase. Employers who refused to increase wages would find their jobs unfilled and those employers would either go out of business because they could not attract workers at the lower wage, or the wage would have to be increased. If there were more supply (of workers) than demand, wages would fall, and the message would go out that that particular industry had an abundance of labor already. Immigration might slow as a result. And the dynamic cycle could continue, always being in balance naturally, without the need for money and laws and fences to restrict immigration. For those who fear "illegal immigration" the solution is simple: Eliminate laws against immigration. Make the problem not a problem.

Instead, our politicians pander to our fear of outsiders by proposing increased border patrols, whose high-speed car chases to track down "offenders" have resulted in the deaths of innocent people in Southern California. What sort of world view concept makes that justifiable? And these old fashioned ideas have been with us for a long time. Over 100 years ago, before the Civil War, the party opposing all immigration into this country was called the American Party, also known appropriately as "The Know-Nothing Party." They feared that immigrants would work for lower wages and therefore hurt "American" jobs. Today, over a century later, our thinking remains the same.

Taoist Approaches

In our current thinking we are concerned about job dislocation. I certainly do not intend to undervalue the significance of this concern; being without work and income is demeaning and leads to many other social and personal abuses. But the "solution" is not to restrict others from seeking employment, which simply does not work. We must instead recognize the problem for what it truly is and then seek real answers.

Of course job disruption is possible, but only when viewed in a regionalized, nationalized context. On a global scale, without lines and boundaries, there might never be a shortage of either goods or services. Labor could flow into industries where the demand was greater. During this transformation, we could provide economic and other assistance for those so displaced, to enable them to regain their competitiveness. This is, again, where the "heart" comes in. A society as vast as that of the United States has money enough to take care of human needs once we eliminate war from our minds and our budgets.

But there is more than just immigration involved in Taoist approaches to these problems. Taoism teaches what might be known in capitalist circles as laissez-faire, which, simply interpreted, means to keep government interference at a minimum. In Taoist terms, it means letting the universe take its natural course and not interfering with its processes. Throughout Taoist thought, less is always more, for by doing less, by letting events work themselves out naturally, we can achieve more. It means allowing these forces to find their own level; when they do, there can be balance and harmony among them. In economic terms, this concept means allowing the natural market forces of supply and demand to operate within a sphere of minimum interference. When supply and demand are in balance, there will be an economic equilibrium, a harmony. There will be enough supply to meet demand. There can be enough jobs for those who want them—not just "American" jobs, but jobs globally.

Economic policies must be developed that let all segments of worldwide society win; this is also the "heart" factor. When we reach the point of harmony and balance, we can have all that we need, and if our views have changed along with our mentality, we can also have all that we want. Having all that we need is enough, by definition. It means we can leave enough for everyone else to have all that they need. It means we need not destroy the planet in the process of getting all that we want.

Left alone, economic conditions can stabilize and find a balance. Over the centuries, we have attempted to control economic conditions, much as we have attempted to control other human conditions. In economic terms, this process of restriction creates artificial markets, with the result that prices are higher overall and, generally, quality is lower, due to lack of competition. We all pay these higher prices and suffer the lower quality so that a small number of companies or individuals can benefit. It is a traditional either/or approach. Letting markets find their balance point naturally, however, through the operation of supply and demand, means that we are acting in accordance with the best interests of the planet as a whole. In the end, money and markets left alone may eventually prevail, just as everything in nature may prevail over human endeavor. As the pressures we exert individually and through government policies begin to relax, and as the natural forces begin to find their own levels, a balance can be found in which we can all find harmony. In practical terms, this means work and monetary, not momentary, satisfaction.

It is our personal, internal definitions, our individual standards, that must change. We are seeking to maintain old standards and ideals, even in the face of changing world conditions. We are no longer the sole monetary powerhouse nation that we once were, and yet we want to get back to that place. We want to war against nations now making inroads into our territory.

Though war is destructive, we seek security in arms. We believe that economic success is equated with continual growth, even though such continual growth has lead us into the very economic and ecological problems we now face. We feel that our pride, both national and personal, is on the line, and we are struggling, through these policies and through our individual conduct, to hold on and control an out-of-control world.

By changing our minds, we can change our economic future. To do this, we will have to let go of our traditional ideas about money, ideas that have lead us to our current state but that we continue to beat to death, thinking that if we only "fine-tune" them, they will begin to work. These are ideas about jobs, about markets, about isms, about nations. Today, in the face of rising unemployment and business failures, in the face of homelessness, drug and alcohol abuse, and gangs, we still focus on the Dow Jones Industrial Average, thinking that somehow the *yang* response to some statistical information is an indicator of how we are doing. We do this because we have done so since the turn of this century, so we keep on doing it. These ideas must be discarded in favor of new ideas that, in essence, amount to a Declaration of Economic Freedom. This Declaration can enable us to pursue new ideas, no matter how radical or different they may seem, simply because they are new. This Declaration of Economic Freedom is integrally intertwined with our ability to be free from war.

What the Declaration means in Taoist terms is that the world of economics must be free to find its own level, must be free to flow and, like water, seek its own balance, its own equilibrium. Our societies are replete with regulations of one sort or another, one restriction or another, one level of pressure or another, all designed to keep the natural laws of economics from operating. We have thousands of tariffs and price supports and import quotas to keep out goods manufactured in other countries. By "we," I mean all nations of the world, each of which operates in the same way. Concepts of nationalism continue to prevail in a time when globalism should be the theme. Each nation is trying to protect its own national jobs, as though each group of jobs were somehow separate and discrete from jobs in other nations. In the zero-sum game we are playing, when someone "wins" another "loses." We pursue economic policies that mirror our fears of the world, and we translate them into money for war (if, indeed, economic war) and none for peace.

All economic barriers should be eliminated. In the same way that there is no reason to go to war, there is no reason to protect ourselves from other countries' economic policies. Tariffs and duties levied against "foreign" goods restrain the freedom of the market-place, especially since it is no longer clear which goods are foreign and which products are global. Price supports such as those for sugar, tobacco, pasta, and nonfat dry milk restrain freedom. Ditches dug across the lines on a map, to keep out foreigners, restrain freedom. All these artificial devices keep prices and wages either higher or lower than if the marketplace were free to find its own level. These devices are as unrealistic as government-controlled markets were in the Communist world. They protect the few against the many; but more importantly, they keep freedom from occurring. To eliminate them, however, would eliminate the interests that have become vested in them over the eons—thus the resistance.

The breakdown of the Soviet empire is evidence that the press of natural forces will eventually overcome the inertia of old ideas, and the more those forces are resisted, the greater the eventual disruption. If we keep out foreign goods, we diminish the income of the people living in those other countries, which in turn causes their economic disruption and diminishes their abilities to buy our goods. It also forms the basis for guerrilla wars to topple what is seen to be the vested interests. The economic barriers that "protect" American businesses are in fact the seeds of their and our destruction.

It is imperative that we begin to see ourselves as part of the entire planet and to understand that there is nothing to run from in the economic arena. It is imperative because clearly, based on the evidence, that is what is happening anyway. The world is homogenizing, and we can either continue to fight and struggle to prevent it, or bend and find ways to go along with the flow. Despite clear indications that these changes are occurring, however, we continue to pretend that they are not. We think that if only we do this or that, we can revive what we think we remember about our glory days.

We do this because there is more light over here than there is where the solution lies.

Principle 5:
Do Not Be Afraid of Monetary Self-Interest

The overriding principle in Taoism is that we must learn to use the natural forces of the universe to achieve our goals. Learning to find the way of least resistance is the key.

Remember the earlier reference to the straw finger traps that were made in occupied Japan after World War II. The only way to free yourself from their grasp was not to pull furiously, for to do so only tightened the trap, but rather to ease the two sides together in order to pull out your fingers. By cooperating with and not fighting against the natural forces represented by the trap, you achieved your goal. When we apply this principle to money, it means that if left alone, natural forces can find the "solution" to the particular problem we face, without the need of extensive and sometimes expensive interference. It means that money, like all other elements, can find its own level, a place of balance and harmony, if left alone or at least with the most minimal of interference.

Naturally, in any given situation, whether in our personal lives or in our collective lives as a nation, as a global community, the answer will vary. But when we get quiet, when we learn to listen to the Tao speaking to us in our hearts, the way is usually abundantly clear, if not necessarily what we want. And because it is not necessarily what we want, we can choose to try to coerce the situation, to "make" it come out the way we want, or we can let go of our attempts at control and go with what is self-evident. The choice we make may depend on how comfortable we are with listening to our souls and not our brains.

The same notion of correct action applies in most external world situations. Truly, we all know what is right once we remove from our thought process all of the baggage that clouds it. One piece of luggage we usually lug out is simply that the idea that might work is new or different, and that, in and of itself, frequently dooms it as a choice. Another such restraint is that we believe only massive government programs can solve problems; we do not realize that many of those problems can be solved by appealing to the more instinctive feelings we all possess.

Taoist thought advocates using the strengths of the problem to overcome the problem's resistance, and thus achieve the goal. The problem may be personal, monetary, or otherwise. Using the strengths of the problem means learning how to find the path of least resistance toward solving it, rather than trying to overcome the problem by force or other coercive actions. In terms of money, sometimes this coercive action takes the form of huge government programs, although doing much less and using the natural forces will sometimes work better. But doing nothing, or doing little, is a difficult concept for us to accept because we have become accustomed to doing something about everything, and we expect our political leaders to act that way.

When I speak of the "strengths of the problem," I also speak of ourselves as the problem. As discussed earlier, we create many of the problems we attribute to outside forces. It is a question of finding our own part in the problem and learning to use our natural forces to overcome our own resistance and the problem.

So many myths, so much baggage exists around the topic of money that sometimes it is difficult to find the solutions to money problems. Having money is a goal for many people, but when they get that money, they are tormented by having it. The use of money for what are deemed selfish purposes is considered self-indulgence and creates its own set of issues. But money is a security device for most of us—and there is nothing wrong in acknowledging, rather than denying, that role.

Therefore, when we are trying to solve money problems, we must recognize that the "strengths" of these particular problems are our own need for self-protection, for self-interest. This may seem paradoxical and conflicting with Taoism, but it is not. Self-interest is instinctive and innate. To deny this is to resist natural forces. Acting in our own self-interest is *wu-wei*, the term used to describe conduct that is in harmony with the natural forces of the universe. To resist is to fail to recognize these interests for what they are. And so we can use the very strengths we have, which are also the sources of the problems we face, to overcome those problems. Using these natural forces can help us eliminate a problem without increasing it by artificial interference, coercion, or control.

Allowing our own self-interest to guide us through a problem is a problem for many of us, however. We feel that neither we nor society is enlightened enough to act with *our* self-interest in mind. Nor do we see how *our* self-interest must be seen as part of everyone's interest.

Acting with self-interest is not an absolute point of view. Like everything else in the universe, our conduct must be relative to all other things, since in nature everything exists only in relationship to all else. Action taken in one area always leads to a response somewhere else. To act with self-interest to the detriment of everyone else is not only anti-Taoist but egocentric, and may ultimately fail to be a satisfactory solution in the long term even for ourselves. Our self-interest depends upon everyone's self-interest. Self-interest in this context means understanding that if one group is maltreated, it will only lead to their resistance and ultimately, over some period of time, to resistance in and breakdown of the whole system.

Therefore, the point is to redefine self-interest, not to deny it. Call it enlightened self-interest, if you will. It is not that everyone's right to succeed must be pooled with everyone else's; rather, in order to truly succeed, in order to truly live at peace, in order to be economically viable as an entire society, solutions have to be those in which everyone wins. This is not to be interpreted as some idealistic morality in which everyone is supposed to rid themselves of possessions and the mindset that creates the need for them. That point of view, even if correct in spirit, currently brings no satisfaction but rather only frustration, for it is, at least today, completely contrary to human nature. It cannot now be applicable on anything but the smallest of scales, if that.

There is no evidence anywhere to be found that everyone, that anyone, is ready to give up acquisition as a way of life. But acquisition alone is not the problem. The problem is acquisition in ways that harm others, either by depriving them of a livelihood or by destroying the planet in the process, or in other antisocial actions. We seem to believe that free market capitalism and altruism are polar opposites, that helping others is to be equated with sacrifice and best to be avoided: the traditional dualistic as opposed to Taoist approach. The choice is not to bemoan this lack of appropriate consumption but rather to learn to use money, self-interest, in a socially acceptable way so that money and acquisitions do not materially impair the welfare of others and the planet as a whole. This is learning how to use the strengths of a problem, in this instance a monetary problem, to solve that problem. The ability to see ourselves in this light comes with personal growth, and with personal growth comes social awareness of the unity of all life.

When we reach a place in our growth in which we learn that money is not who we are, when we discover our connection to all things and how we fit, then we can let go of our need to acquire to the exclusion of everyone else. Our value systems then may have changed, so that we have everything that we need without needing everything we see. Our self-interest then can be seen as integrally involved with everyone's self-interest. If enough of us reach that place, cooperation and not confrontation can be the natural force.

To draw the circle a bit closer, the earlier example of each of us driving gasoline-guzzling cars is self-interest to the detriment of the planet as a whole. If our purpose in driving such cars is to help define ourselves as individuals, make us feel better about ourselves, then I suggest it is the definition that needs examination, for it makes us unwilling to cooperate with the natural forces, thereby leading to all the symptoms about which I have spoken.

These are our goals—but we are clearly not there yet, and so the decisions we make today about solving our monetary and money-related social problems must accommodate the reality of self-interest. In order to effect this sort of change, we cannot attempt to redo human nature. Instead we must learn to appeal to the most selfish of instincts, which, in terms of business, are money and profit. Unless those who must change find a compelling reason to do so, the inertia that is resistance to change will overcome any such reasons. In our personal lives, the forces that compel change are crises: divorce, the death of a loved one, illness, loss of a job. In the world of business, too, the compelling force may be a crisis, such as toxic waste finally hitting home on the balance sheet. The force may also be the need to become or remain competitive in the marketplace or go out of business.

Let me give an example: When the Berlin Wall crumbled, amidst the rubble of what once was we saw the effects of the pressures of deutsch marks, of pounds sterling, of yens, and of U.S. dollars, which were largely responsible for the crumbling. Though ideology clearly played a part in the process, I suggest that the real cause of the rapid change that occurred and is still occurring was money and the lack thereof. Money in this case is defined in its broadest sense, to include not only actual money and the bread and clothes it can buy, but the modern age and its major changes in the way the industrialized world thinks and, more importantly, communicates. Money includes television, which brought to the people behind the Iron Curtain a picture of better cars, travel, computers—and a higher standard of living based upon what people in the former Eastern Bloc saw as being enjoyed by people in the West.

Every society wants essentially what the most advanced societies have. There are all sorts of western products now available throughout the world. This is not to say that this phenomenon is either good or bad, but only that it exists. And it exists because, in an open society, people want these goods and services. This, too, is self-interest, and rather than resisting this self-interest by building walls to keep out such products, a government can govern best by simply letting such self-interest find its natural place in the society. Thus, in the long run, economics can serve as a median, a common ground, to homogenize away the cultural differences that have led to war. To bemoan what works is to be overly caught up in the ism. Accepting what works opens up new ideas, and if preserving culture is one of them, then rather than fight against the flow, there are other ways of achieving that goal so that everyone wins.

What must occur if change is to be profitable is that the process must not only be painless for individuals on the buying end but good for business on the selling end. And what is required is the mindset to accomplish this. It is change that comes about from the profit (self-interest) motivation. One such example today is that we have "dolphin-safe tuna" and other "green" and "environmentally friendly" goods on our supermarket shelves. This is self-interest being turned to the good.

This is an example of using the freedom of the marketplace and the concept of the connectedness of all seemingly isolated issues, to actually solve problems by catering to our self-interest, by "yielding to the enemy," if you will.

Business is nothing more than our personal self-interests wearing three-piece suits. And our self-interests must be modified to respond to the concept of freedom in the marketplace. It would be nice to expect people to do for others simply for the good of doing for others, but it may never be successful as a policy. There must, at least for the present, be a method of showing the giver what's in it for him or her. The agenda to help others less fortunate must also include self-interest.

Some Specifics

Suppose that, instead of fixed salaries, our key elected officials, from Congress to the President, were paid on commission. Give them an incentive plan, a piece of the action, as it were. I suspect that pork-barreling, budget deficits, special interest legislation, price supports for agricultural products, and excessively high and outrageous military spending would, in one instant, end. We should amend the Constitution to provide for this approach to federal government efficiency. This same idea might also be used at every level of government.[1]

This is how it can work: Economists would get together and establish a viable set of norms for a "floor" —a base year or other statistic—that reflects an overall state of economic health for the country. Perhaps it would be the gross domestic product, or a reduction of the budget deficit, or some other equally arcane set of criteria that would be used for determining the state of the nation's economic prosperity. (Hopefully, given enough enlightenment, that criteria would be more encompassing than those used now.) Using that statistic, a formula could then be developed whereby officials who are most able to influence economic spending would have their salaries pegged to a change in that statistic. Each official would be in a position to make a substantially higher salary and bonus if the goal for that statistic were surpassed, or a much lower one if it were not. Programs that directly affect the poor, the elderly, the underprivileged and the like, such as Social Security, education programs, welfare, and so on, would be exempt from the formula.

Not only might this system attract successful and highly motivated businesspeople into government, instead of the unimaginative political types who now populate the system, but it might also eliminate wasted expenditures; our budget deficit and consequent economic prosperity might improve measurably. We would probably not have to worry about our legislators taking favors from special interest groups because the legislators could make much more money voting for efficiency.

With an improved economy, more money could then be spent to help the underprivileged—who today must get little or nothing because, they are told, there is simply not enough to go around. We could find enough money to improve public education, pave roads, and support alternative energies that do not kill us as we use them. A more profitable operation all around benefits everyone.

Another example: The United States is, at this writing, one of the few industrialized countries without some sort of national and comprehensive health care system. When our population ages into the next century, this situation is going to get significantly worse, as all of the baby-boomers reach their older years, and fewer workers are in the system to pay taxes. The over-75 population is expected to increase substantially over the next 10 to 15 years, and health care costs are expected to rise in equal proportion. Consequently, there is much talk about establishing some sort of national health care system. But these current plans depend either on (1) raising taxes to help those who will not be able to pay for their own coverage (even though we are told that a general tax increase is not part of the proposals); (2) limiting costs in the form of insurance company rate increases and doctor and hospital charges (especially from Medicare for the elderly —thereby pitting this group against the rest of us and creating, as a result, a source for the self-destruction of the plan), and/or rationing health care itself.

Also involved is the creation of yet another huge and expensive governmental program, which we all pay for whether we get benefits or not. Indeed, at the time of this writing, under President Clinton's health care proposal, the United States government would have to throw its considerable weight behind *encouraging* smoking in order to raise enough money via this "sin" tax to pay for the "health" care of the rest of us. If smoking actually declines, the house of cards that is the President's plan falls completely apart. In short, these plans require coercion instead of cooperation, regulation instead of freedom. They are inconsistent with Taoist and, indeed, with free-market ideas.

Expecting the elderly to pay for their own health care is not going to work, since most of them cannot afford to pay under the meager Social Security payments they receive. A few years ago, just such a proposal (for catastrophic care) was repealed because of opposition from the elderly. Most younger taxpayers are unwilling to pay higher taxes because they will not be the immediate recipients of the aid, and no one wants to pay now for something they might or might not receive 40 years down the road. So we have a "crisis" in health care.

It turns out that we do not have a health care crisis, however; we have yet another crisis of vision, as indeed we have about nearly every one of the problems we as a society face. The "crisis" is created because we are again trying to solve a problem by the wrong means. As a result, we have not even made a dent in the problem, nor are we ever likely to as long as we continue to approach the "solution" with the same skewed point of view.

Our approach has been to legislate that doctors and hospitals treat the elderly and infirm for all illnesses, including catastrophic ones. We have created expensive Medicare-type programs that do not pay anywhere near the cost of treatment. These programs are funded by taxes—across-the-board taxes that we all pay, and taxes levied in the form of deductibles and co-payments on the elderly and infirm, neither of which group is able to pay their share. As a result, doctors and hospitals do not receive full payment for their services. Some hospitals have failed entirely, or at least are out of the trauma business, because they cannot afford to stay open and treat patients without adequate compensation. In turn, the elderly and infirm receive poor-quality care or sometimes no care at all, either because they are not being treated or because they cannot afford their share of insurance premiums, or both. Those who pay taxes to support this system object because they do not receive any of the benefits, such as they are; these taxpayers generally have their own insurance, and whatever benefits are available are in the future. As a result, no one wins and everyone loses.

Good medical care is expensive, given the cost of new diagnostic equipment, drugs, and so on. U.S. physicians and hospitals will probably not want to scale down their standard of living or reduce their incomes to help those who cannot pay for their services. This is the effect of trying to limit costs. To expect that they would is naive and completely contrary to human nature. The Tao does not suggest this as a viable approach.

A better approach is one that requires another point of view, one that caters and indeed panders to the self-interest of everyone—for that is the only way it is going to work. Given that it seems to be the natural way, it is consistent with Taoism.

We should, accordingly, revise the tax laws and, instead of paying them, give doctors and hospitals double or triple or quadruple deductions for treating those who are within a defined needy class, such as the elderly, the uninsured, and the poor. We already have much by way of special-interest tax legislation, so this is not in and of itself a ground-breaking concept. What is important here is that it provides the medical community with the necessary self-interest to provide the services, and it does not raise taxes on the population as a whole, to which circumstance there is great resistance. Doctors and hospitals would probably welcome such patients in order to reduce their taxes by a multiple of their costs. At the same time, those who could afford it could still have their private insurance, thereby giving doctors and hospitals a continued stream of real income. Everyone wins.

Needless to say, there will be much screaming that we are favoring the rich doctors again. The response, of course, is that this "favoring" is done in a holistic fashion, in a way that benefits the entirety of society. Certainly there are many existing favorable tax treatments and public giveaways in which only those being favored win and everyone else loses, such as price supports for agricultural products, tariffs on competing foreign goods, weapons spending, and so on. At least under this health-care tax deduction proposal, the benefits serve the common good.

Many will say that we cannot afford to reduce government's income by reducing taxes; after all, we already have a large deficit. But of course we can. It is a question of rethinking priorities and acting not out of fear of Them, but as members of humanity. Clearly, the apparently bottomless pit of money spent on war could be simply reallocated. Our tax revenues available for expenditures of other sorts would then be higher by that amount of money, and might be enough to compensate for those lost payments from the medical or business community—even if taxes remain the same. Alternatively, we could reduce significantly the tax burden we all share by the same amount that we now spend on war, or at least by the difference between that amount and the loss of income from the aforesaid deductions.[2]

Another example: If we are truly interested in reducing our great social problems (and it is by no means clear that we are, rhetoric to the contrary notwithstanding), then, as I have said, we must deal with root causes. This means dealing with the complete lack of self-respect that causes self-abuse. Part of this lack of self-esteem comes from joblessness, both for teens as well as their parents. When the various administrations over the past decade have cut from U.S. budgets money for support of families and school lunch programs, it is little wonder that the result has been hungry and deprived children turning to gangs and crime seeking the "self-esteem" they lack. Recall the examples given before about this same sort of behavior taking place in third-world countries burdened by heavy debt.

Because we may actually fear the rising strength of the minorities whose plight we talk of championing, we resist higher taxes to pay for programs that would benefit them. We elect leaders who, given the slightest opportunity, cut these programs. These leaders reflect our own prejudices. And yet we scream out for change, especially when we begin to feel the impact of crime, and drug abuse, and reduced market competitiveness due to substandard public education. But any proposal directly requiring higher taxes for the purpose of helping those who seem unable to help themselves appears doomed, for at least the foreseeable future, until our viewpoint changes drastically.

One approach entirely consistent with Taoist self-interest is to provide what have been called "enterprise zones" for businesses. Tax laws can be changed to offer to any business that opens a factory or store in a designated depressed area, employing, say, 200 or so minority employees and paying, say, x dollars per hour, benefits such as double or triple tax deductions, faster depreciation, and the like. What can happen is that the factories open, jobs become available, skills are learned, children see their parents working and being able to provide, and this in turn can lead to those children's respect for parents as role models, which might spill over into self-respect for both the parents and the children. Unemployment might be reduced significantly, gang and drug wars might cease to be of value to the disaffected. Working brings in more money than welfare. Everyone wins and no one loses.

The idea of enterprise zones has been advanced before, but our traditional approach has been to throw small amounts of money into such programs because we need the rest for war, and so the programs fail. Even though many government leaders advocate such programs, the government never provides enough money and time to make them work. Everyone loses and no one wins.

Are these ideas radical? Perhaps. Naive? Only because they are new and untried. The key to adopting these policies and others like them is to understand that we must operate not out of fear, but out of certainty that with openness and cooperation, fear and mistrust can be eliminated. Fear means not just fear of military attack, but fear that there is scarcity in the world, that unless we get ours, someone else will get it, whatever "it" is. The key is having a view of the world as an integrated system, one that cannot operate at all unless each of its component parts is operating. If some of those parts are deprived, malnourished, hungry, repressed, at war, then the system is not operating for all and inequities will continue to exist. If you will think, in your own imagination, what you would do to change the world if you had the opportunity, you will probably find that these notions are similar to yours. These ideas are founded upon a humanistic, philosophical, and conceptual framework, yet are concrete and achievable.

The way to eliminate a whole host of "problems" is to make them "nonproblems." The way to do this is to open our minds to new ideas about the "problems," so that we seek solutions that work because they follow the natural energies of the universe. In the example of money and economics, the natural forces are self-interest. Furthermore, individual responsibility is the key, and if all the new policies are based upon a sense that individual worth or the lack of it is at the heart of both the problem and the solution, then the context will be clear. The core of these ideas is the concept of relationships, both personal as well as international. With a firm sense of belief in ourselves as individuals as well as a collective society, we can achieve anything.

Thus the circle is drawn. Until we accept that we have no enemies that require huge expenditures on war, until we decide to reallocate our resources toward dealing with what is truly an affront to our security, approaches such as those I have put forth go nowhere. Changes in the real world require extensive changes in our views of that world and, in turn, extensive changes in our views of ourselves in relationship to others on the planet. "The Taoist moral is that people who mistrust themselves and one another are doomed."[3]

Principle 6:
We Are Still at War

In as real a sense as we can imagine, all of us are victims of war. Our individual plights, which may seem to be only about money, can, if we are willing to go deep enough, be traced directly to our spending on war and the mindset that allows us to war in the first place.

We are at war within ourselves because we are not at peace with ourselves. And because we are not at peace, we remain torn and confused about the role money plays in our lives and our use of it for self-destruction. And because we are personally confused, we are collectively confused. The world is, after all, only all of us added up.

We remain at war despite the ostensible peace. We mark the artificial end of one war without realizing that all we have done is seed the fertile ground for the next. Since we began we have been in a continuous state of war—with other nations and within our own house. We are at war with the poor, the uneducated, children, people with AIDS, the elderly. We are at war with our own environment, dying not from without but from within.

As is everything else that is in transition, we are facing a world in which traditional ideas, like traditional enemies, are (or should be) changing. Our ideas about war should be changing so that we can align ourselves with the natural forces of the universe, as described in the Tao. Unfortunately, it is clear that we are not doing so.

It seems evident that the only way to achieve peace and economic stability, secure jobs, ensure competitiveness in world markets, gain freedom from fear of economic disaster, enhance self-respect, eliminate substance abuse along with the panoply of other great social ills we all face, is to eliminate war. This is the practical, real-world way in which we can let go of the control, the coercion over external events that we think we need and have. It is through the mechanisms of war that humankind has attempted to exert that control. And the connection between money and war is apparent, so it seems appropriate in a book dealing with the spirituality of money to talk about its connection to war.

> Businessmen . . . opt for war when they have
> exhausted their home markets and have nowhere
> else to sell their wares.[1]

None of the great social ills our nation faces—
crime in our streets, lack of education in our schools,
poverty and homelessness in our cities, lack of health
care for tens of millions of us, lack of competitiveness
in foreign markets—none of those problems nor any
others will ever be solved as long as we remain at war.
Not only have we diverted vast sums of money for war,
monies that could be used to solve these problems,
but our war mentality has caused us to see these problems in inappropriate ways. Spending money on the
military is our chief symptom of being at war, but war
is also a state of mind, regardless of whether actual
battles are being fought. War is an internal phenomenon that spreads its tentacles into the societal problems we claim we want to cure.

As a result of our lack of vision, of our separateness from others, we are using our money to harm, not
to heal. That same separateness prevents us from
seeing creative approaches to other social problems
because we do not view ourselves as any part of their
cause.

The Tao stands for achieving that which is sought
through cooperation—not through confrontation with
the natural forces. War is neither a means nor an end.

> Only Nature knows the proper time for a man to
> die.
> To kill is to interrupt Nature's design for
> dying. . . .[2]

War represents old thinking. It is no longer (if ever it was) a viable means of resolving disputes. War represents old ideas in a time when new ideas are required.

Understand that I am not talking about traditional calls for nonviolence, although nonviolence is at the core of Taoism and at the deepest part of a soul at peace. Rather, what the Tao speaks of is *avoiding violence*, avoiding the conditions that lead to violence and war, by avoiding and obviating the reasons we go to war—before they become so compelling that nothing else, no other solution seems workable. Taoism teaches us to see problems before they become violent. Taoism tells us that to solve a problem we cannot force a solution, as through war, but rather we must learn to make the problem a nonproblem, so that we do not have to try and control it.

Critics will, I am certain, be quick to put forth situations in history when resorting to war seemed the only way out. But Taoism tries to give us a different way of looking at things, a way in which the underlying causes that led to our need to resort to war are dealt with before they reached the crisis stage. As I said in an earlier discussion about Gulf War I, during the many years leading up to the war, if society had changed any of its points of view along the way, we might have obviated the killing and destruction that followed. The same can be said of virtually every war.

What Does Warmoneywar Look Like?

While we all loudly protest that we do not want war, we conduct ourselves directly to the contrary. We spend obscene amounts of money on war and its preparations and on the results of war. Despite significant changes in world politics, we continue to spend nearly $300 billion annually on our military (when money allocated for the Department of Energy, interest on the national debt related to previous military expenditures, and other such items are included). Current proposals involve spending in excess of a trillion dollars over the next five years on our military machine, even after factoring in small and incremental cuts. Imagine that: over a *trillion* dollars!

We were told and we believed that while the Soviet Union was together as a nation and presented itself as a solid threat, we needed to spend these sums on our "defense."

Now we are told and we believe that because the Soviet Union has fallen apart and is no longer together as a nation, we still need to spend these sums on "defense" because the new nations spawned of the U.S.S.R. represent a series of new potential threats.

And we have invented new enemies to justify this continued high level of military spending. Small nations and regional conflicts have been raised to "enemy" status. So we can never win. These are other examples of our not thinking for ourselves and simply following the ideas of government leaders, about which I wrote earlier.

We continue to build missiles and submarines and weapons systems that serve no purpose in today's world. Even as we proclaim significant cutbacks in nuclear missiles between our nation and Russia, we remain committed to enormous spending programs designed to build even more missiles and submarines. We spent between $30 and $35 billion on the "Star Wars" or Strategic Defense Initiative program, which program has now simply been refocused on other missile systems. We have spent or will spend nearly $45 billion to build the B-2 bomber, whose sole selling point was that it could evade radar. Though tests have shown that it will not evade radar, we continue to spend money building it.

Continued spending of money in this way deprives us of money for schools. As our federal government launches money at missiles, it loses its ability to share its revenue with local and state governments, which in turn have less money to spend on education. Without spending for war, federal taxes could be reduced significantly, enabling the states to raise taxes for schools or allowing us individually to decide how to fund our children's education. The results of war are that teachers' salaries are being cut and strikes are threatened—even in the face of continually dismal test scores. Fewer and fewer of today's teachers want to teach, and fewer and fewer students opt for teaching as a profession, the rewards being slim indeed. So we end up with a poorly educated work force, no longer able to compete in world markets, which leads us to create enemies of the countries doing better than we economically, which leads to the need to guard against them and to make weapons of war to be used against them . . . and the cycle continues. War creates its own reality.

Continued spending of money in this way deprives us of money for needed health care. Local hospitals arc closing their doors to indigents and the elderly, who are most in need of care, because we and the government lack funds to support those hospitals.[3] The result of war is that we develop an underclass of ill people, whom we consider to be disease-ridden, so desperate for medical attention for themselves and their children that they turn to drugs and crime to acquire enough money. We see stories on the news about how these people have to make choices between whether to eat or to live, because we relegate many of our older citizens to minimal survival pensions even as health care costs soar.

We see television pictures of those who are starving in Africa, where mothers have to make choices about which of their children will receive their skimpy amounts of breast milk, knowing that those choices may lead to another child's death. We think those choices do not have to be made here. But the choices are here too, even if different in kind. We do not understand how much of the starvation and killing rampant in these nations is but a holdover from our own cold war with the Soviet Union. The guns used by the present combatants are the guns either we or our enemy provided when we attempted to divide up the world, not unlike Spain and Portugal centuries ago.

Continued spending of money in this way reduces our ability to creatively handle the problems —all the social ills, such as violence and poverty— that a positive, holistic society should simply not tolerate. The results of war are that we allow these problems to grow to such large proportions that we then turn to repressive measures, attempting to "cure" the ills, which in turn breeds more antisocial activity, which leads to even harsher measures . . . and the cycle continues.

Over the years, our fears of "the enemy" created a war machinery that threatens to destroy the ecology of the very nation it was supposed to protect. Estimates today are that it will take hundred of billions of dollars just to clean up the toxic mess created by these war facilities, and a total as high as $1.7 trillion for all our waste cleanup. The results of war are that we are killing ourselves and others on the planet, without a single shot being fired.

The United States is the largest supplier of military arms to third-world nations, even as we proclaim our desire to limit such sales. In the name of promoting "world peace," our government sells weapons of war to other governments, even to those in turmoil. Western governments refuse to restrict sales of nuclear technology, even as the spread of nuclear weapons threatens us all. Despite Pakistan's refusal to sign the Nuclear Nonproliferation Treaty, and that country's expressed acknowledgment that it has a nuclear weapons capability, we sold arms to that nation.

Our leaders have always told us that there is not enough money for programs to help people directly, and yet there is always enough for war. It is the same with virtually every industrialized nation in the world.

Warmoneywar is about the integral connection between war and money and war. *Warmoneywar* is also about profits and war-related jobs which have been and remain the causes of war and spending on war. Even with recent cutbacks, millions of U.S. citizens are directly employed in the military industry and in related industries. Congress refuses to cut back on military spending for fear people will lose their jobs

and politicians will lose elections. As a result, one segment of our society is employed in an unneeded war-
making capacity, and we are paying their salaries.

Though it is certainly true that severe reductions
in military spending will create further unemployment, when looked at from a Taoist viewpoint such
individual disruptions do not alter the fundamental
truths about unity and peace. Those who are affected
directly protest that the only way to save jobs is to continue to build war machines. We have created industries that kill, and people's lives have become vested
with the fruits of such industries, but that does not
mean we should allow their harmful existence to continue merely to protect those jobs. What we have
believed are vested interests are only temporary and
are not immutable. The ebb of those industries is part
of the *yin* and *yang* of the universe, and adaptation—
with government assistance, not codependency—is
the answer. We can transform what we have come to
believe as vested into more healthful occupations.
Taoism insists that the health of the entire society be
considered.

War Is More than Just Money

There is more to the problem of war than just the
money we spend on it. Humankind has a war men-

tality. In the United States, we have had a perpetual enemy for as long as we have been a nation. England, Germany, Japan, Mexico, Cuba, Nicaragua, Native Americans, "Communist" rebels in El Salvador, "Communist" rebels in Grenada, "Communist" rebels in the Dominican Republic, "Communist" rebels in Guatemala, "Communist" rebels in Namibia, "Communist" rebels in Chile, Spain, Italy, the Soviet Union, North Korea, North Vietnam, Iran, Iraq, Libya, and China all have been our "enemy." And because we have grown up with another enemy, in the form of scarcity, we accept their statement when our political leaders tell us who the current enemy is.

We are willing to believe it to be so in the larger world, hence we see enemies in our personal world as well. The weakness of our souls feeds the outer-world weakness, which is war. We see enemies in other people and groups who are different from us, who want rights for themselves that we feel will deprive us of rights. The relationship between our views of our outer and inner worlds resonates with us and thus makes that relationship credible. It becomes self-fulfilling. This thinking is both the root of how we see the larger world and the cause of how we see our own world.

Sometimes the signs we are at war are so subtle and so ingrained that we do not even think about them. When a head of state travels to Washington or visits another country, the host country may offer a parade of soldiers as part of the protocol. A 21-gun salute is considered appropriate. This harks back to medieval times, when to do so was a show of force designed to intimidate the opponent. We still continue this practice: We are still at war, even with our friends.

At the conclusion of Gulf War I, there was a huge ticker-tape parade in New York. An estimated 6,000 tons of paper was hurled out windows to celebrate our victorious forces. A gala, called a memorial, was held inside the cathedral of St. John the Divine. What scattered protesters were able to sneak in were forcibly ejected, to show how much in favor of peace we were. We celebrated our glorious victory while pretending we did not glory in victory.

On December 7, 1991, the fiftieth anniversary of the bombing of Pearl Harbor, we allowed ourselves to become transfixed by images of war. All over our television screens were visuals of Japanese planes dive-bombing and strafing U.S. warships. This media diversion took our minds off our then-current economic and social decline. It reminded us yet again that we have an "enemy," this time an economic one, but an "enemy" nonetheless. We demanded an apology from the Japanese for their attack, but we refuse to apologize for our nuclear attack on Hiroshima and Nagasaki. The implication was that They started the war, and We were justified in killing 200,000 people to end it. We were told that we held the moral high ground ("high ground" being another image from war) and, because we constantly look for any way to boost our declining stature in the world, we allowed our collective national ego to rule. Japan bashing was and remains quite fashionable.

Our war mentality has allowed our leaders to pervert the Constitution that we contend we fight for, by engaging us in numerous wars without Congress ever declaring them. U.S. soldiers have been killed in Korea and in Vietnam, in Lebanon and in Panama, without a declaration of war. We glorify war even to the point of violating the very basis for the democracy we claim to defend.

We define ourselves by our enemies. We are the "good guys" and They are the "bad guys." We stand for freedom, and They stand for oppression. We thus have a *raison d'être*, a reason for being, a place to put our insecurities. After the Soviets passed from the scene as the credible bogeyman, along came Iraq, or drugs, or some other demon to take Russia's place. We fight wars over money, as well, to define our identity. On the economic battlefield, we are the victors or the vanquished. We are the oppressors or the oppressed. They are going to take what is ours: our automobile industry, our garment factory jobs, our welfare. It is either Them or Us; we are either/or and nothing more. The lines are clearly drawn, and in our need for a world of certainty, this makes sense to us. Without war, it is hard to tell who are the winners and the losers, and this lack of clarity is hard for us to handle.

We cannot alter who we are until we alter war as a reality, but we will not alter war because we think to do so means altering the very essence of who we are. As long as there is war, we will never have that opportunity for change, because accepting war means accepting the status quo. For those bound to dualistic thinking, this leads us back to only what we know, which is war. We cannot think our way out of the problem until we alter how we think.

Recently, at a hearing on airport noise abatement held at the request of homeowners complaining about late-night jet takeoffs, new rules were adopted limiting those flights to certain hours. But military flights were exempted. If the military was involved, the noise was somehow acceptable. Exactly what urgent military necessity would require such midnight flights from a suburban airport is difficult to imagine. These are further examples of how we behave when we do not think for ourselves, when we follow the stampeding crowd.

A more refined and enlightened viewpoint would require us to ask *what* exactly is the "nation" we are so willing to die for? What *are* the monetary

and economic boundaries of this nation? Are geopolitical maps such as the kind we grew up with even
meaningful today, in a world where businesses cross
these lines every minute of the day? In today's world,
it makes little sense to waste lives over yesterday's
ideas.

We cannot expect to end crime in our cities when
we commit crimes on other nations, even though—
because we band together, wear uniforms, and call it
war—our crimes take on a heroic quality. We cannot
expect to end pollution by individuals when collectively, in the name of "national security," we have created some of the worst pollution sites in the world. We
cannot expect to end discrimination when our government sanctions such discrimination in its treatment of the underprivileged of the world. It was but
50 years ago that the United States imprisoned
Japanese Americans.

We elect leaders who we know lie to us, kill others
in our name, and build weapons of obscene power,
and then we turn to our children and expect them to
behave differently. We ask them, as it were, to do as
we say not as we do. It is our role, government's role,
to lead by example and not be hypocritical. Today we
are leading by example—but in a perverse way.

War is about money. As a result of our war mentality, proposals offered by our leaders to cut military
spending are irrelevant, for what the politicians are

trying to do is make the smallest reductions possible while still retaining a war-fighting capability. We talk about changes only on the periphery, leaving the central concept of war unaltered in our minds.

Taoist Alternatives

A new approach lies in changing our internal points of view about *warmoneywar*, to see that we are all part of the same problem. Then the cry for war against the external enemy may no longer go out, for we may see that there is no external enemy. Ending our idolatry for war can only happen when we stop being at war within ourselves. For this, change is required not on the outside but on the inside. For this, we must be at peace within ourselves. And as I have stated earlier, coming to a place of peace about money is part of coming to that general peace we must attain.

The argument against war cannot be made with the force of logic alone; it must also be based upon faith and on an attempt to find a new way of seeing the world and the relationships in it. "[The] basic good sense in the Taoist view [is] that we *must* [emphasis supplied] make the desperate gamble of trusting ourselves and others."⁴ We are currently stuck in the old way of looking at the world. We will never be able to eliminate war until we break free of that outmoded point of view and advance ourselves with a new vision, one based on connections rather than separations. Lines on a map reflect lines in our minds. We are forever returning to the concept of scarcity. And this scarcity is related directly and indirectly to a scarcity of money, which is related directly and indirectly to a scarcity of emotional security.

It is not only our country that is dominated by this sort of thinking. Every other warlike nation on Earth operates the same way; and none of them, yet all of them, are to blame for the state of the world, since we all react to one another. Each nation's conduct is both the cause and the effect of every other nation's conduct. We are all in a relationship one to the other. As long as we are separate, we will always be insecure, because there will always be something wanted on one side of some line by the nation on the other side. We are one another's *yin* and *yang*, serving to define one another's existence and justify one another's conduct. We can, however, turn this relationship from being deadly to being healthy.

If the planet is viewed as one unit, then there is no separation, no lack of security, no need for war. This is not merely some "we-are-all-one" philosophy. This unity is in fact the reality, and separateness is the fiction. Consider the world today: What happens in one part of the globe deeply affects every other part. Products are made everywhere. Look at the map of the world not in terms of geopolitical boundaries, and see it based instead upon the reach of transnational corporations. That map then looks very different. See it in terms of ecological destruction across the lines we have drawn, and the map looks very different. A decline in the currency of one country affects tourism in another. What is happening today in the economic realm in Europe, in North America is all about merging separate nations into a single unit, thereby forever eliminating war as an option, for war in that circumstance would be war against oneself. But we still have that third-grader's map of the Earth burned into our minds.

What is going on today is simply a redefinition of the world. True, it is happening very slowly, and we do not speak of it in Taoist terms, to be sure. But the world is slowly finding out, against its will it seems, that war makes no sense. France fought Germany many times over the centuries and is now embraced within the European Economic Community next to its traditional enemy. The Confederation of Independent States, long the enemy of nearly everyone when it was the U.S.S.R., is now a member of The Group of Seven economic pact. Vietnam promotes tourism to rebuild its war-torn economy. In the march toward a free trade agreement between our nation and Mexico, the Alamo has long been forgotten.

These are just a few examples of the natural economic forces of the Tao overcoming the eons of coercion in the form of war. By eliminating war—the actual killing, destructive war as well as the spending of our money in preparation for and as the result of it —we can give ourselves the chance for a new society. By recognizing that these monetary changes are taking place and going along with them instead of continuing to resist them, we can cooperate with instead of confront these natural forces. If we had known that, 20 years after the Vietnam War, throwing a few dollars into the discussion over that country and opening it up to Western visitors with cameras and loud-colored shorts could have prevented the death of hundreds of thousands of people on both sides, would that have ended the conflict? Today in Bosnia and Northern Ireland, although the roots of those conflicts lie in religious differences, differences are even now being expressed in terms of money and jobs and rights in the society. Why do we not recognize these issues and work toward bringing everyone up to economic par, instead of sending guns and tanks and mortars to further the killing?

We Need a Totally New Point of View

Because our basic premise is faulty, we can never eliminate war. Unless we are prepared to accept that *no* war is justified, then *all* wars can be justified. Unless we are prepared to accept that *no* war is justified, then arguing against nuclear weapons, or chemical weapons, or the Strategic Defense Initiative, or this or that advanced weapons system costing x billions, is wasted. The argument says: "We accept war as inevitable and as a part of human nature, but we should fight it with less than the best weapons available to us. We should, in truth, not fight to win." This argument contradicts the rational thought process, and minds will not be changed unless some appeal to rationality can be found. If we accept war as a viable means of dealing with conflict, then logic tells us that we had better do our best to win that war—and that means using every weapon available to us. To try and convince others of a viewpoint with a faulty underlying assumption is a dead-end discussion.

So if war is a given, there is nothing else to talk about, because war in its broadest sense defines every part of our culture and society, whether or not war is related directly to fighting and killing. War not only pits nations against nations but individuals against individuals, each vying for a share of the very-diminished economic pie left over after the costs of war. And each war justifies other wars and is justified by the last war.

Today, people suffering the effects of poverty and hunger and lack of education are the victims of war. They will remain so, because there will never be enough money or resources or will to eliminate those problems as long as there is war. Oppression will continue, for there will always be those in any group or society who will want things the rest are unwilling to give or grant—things like land, or food, or education, or rights roughly equivalent to those whose lives they seek to emulate. In our zero-sum world, where the existing view is of ourselves as individuals separate from the whole, when someone has another must lack. So war continues. And as long as war continues, all of the possibilities of change remain stifled.

We have come to accept, since war has been around seemingly from the beginning, that we as a species are aggressive, warlike, prone to destruction. The only real evidence to support this proposition is the fact of war itself, a sort of hoisting-oneself-by-one's-bootstraps kind of argument. But look where this argument, that we are inherently a warlike species, takes us. It tells us that we are self-destructive. It tells us that we are destined to die. We are self-defeating, in that we can never truly ever be at peace because we are born to die. This argument denies the value of each of us as loving, caring human beings. It reduces us to nothing but animals and denies us the right to use our hearts and our minds to find another way.

In this masculine-dominated world, the male point of view, represented by the *yang*, prevents us from acknowledging that we also have a female, *yin*, side. If we need another (in this case, another nation) to make us whole, to provide oil, to tell us who we are by giving us terms in which we can define our struggle and sacrifice, then we must control that other (nation) so that we feel secure through that control. But we never get to that place of security because we know in truth that at any moment our control over that nation could cease. So we build more weapons to make ourselves feel more secure, the other nation acts in the same way, and so on. The more we feel our security is dependent upon another, the less secure we feel.

War is made by men and women who embody masculine thinking, who do not wish to seem dependent upon another nation for anything. We should be free to take it all. We think that "real" men, and now women who seek combat roles, must be seen as being in control of every situation.

To say, as the Tao says, that we must not use force to conquer the universe, seems to go against the very nature of man's definition of himself. Presidents, the Congress (which is male-dominated even when women representatives are elected) cannot be seen as passive and allowing things to take their natural course. They must be seen as aggressive in the face of aggression. Such is the nature of politics. Politics is not about peace. Politics is about getting elected.

So we must talk about a world without war, and in order to do that, all of us must first come to a place of peace within ourselves, so that we have no reason to go to war against anyone else. This is the essence of life, of personal growth and the reason for our being. Should it ever happen that we get to that place in our deepest selves, we may see solutions that now we cannot see because we are bound by the walls of old ideas. As long as any one of us has not yet reached that pinnacle of growth, war will continue because that one person will keep the fires going.

In order to end war, we must each grow. But in order to grow, each of us must be given the right opportunities, the right amount of food and money and education and chances in life, to build self-esteem. We must understand that our own lives will not be made better or worse by our taking things from others, but only as a result of our own self-love. Disparate economic and social conditions in our individual lives are as much a cause of war as any invasion. The connection between war and money, money and war, is all-pervasive.

Nothing out there will change—whether it be in the state of nuclear arsenals; whether it be in the lack of progress in ending prejudice and bigotry of races, religions, or sexes; whether it be cleaning up the ever-growing level of toxic wastes being generated each day; whether it be in developing alternative ways of resolving our inevitable differences of ideologies short of killing—nothing will be altered unless we begin to take personal responsibility for our lives. Each of those problems is but the symptom of a lack of good feeling about ourselves, extrapolated onto the larger canvas.[5]

What Keeps Us from Changing?

War, the preparation for it, the spending for it, and the mentality that breeds it prevent opportunities for growth. We transfer our war thinking from the foreign battlefield to the home front, the enemy becoming those who we think want our scarce resources. The killing goes on in monetary ways, by our depriving the enemy of jobs and education and health care. When we need to reduce our budget deficits because we have spent so much on war, we turn first to those less-powerful groups in our society and take food (money) out of their mouths.

Thus we cannot grow when there is war, and there will always be war as long as we are not allowed to grow. It seems a vicious cycle, and it is. Our visions breed reality and the reality convinces us that our visions are correct. That reality tells us that our world view is correct because we have sought ratification in the real world based upon our visions. But we can break the cycle—only by breaking our old visions, not the reality. This is so because our individual views constitute the real world, and we cannot expect to impose change from the outside.

A leap of faith is required to overcome this faulty thinking; it will not come via a rational argument, despite all attempts, including this one, to do so. In order to achieve this faith, we must feel secure about our individual selves, so that the demagoguery that incites us to war against others will no longer play into our own insecurities. Self-worth is *the* answer to war, and because of the close connection between war, money, and self-esteem, new ideas about money are an integral, if only one, part of that self-worth.

And so the choice is between living in fear, trying to control everyone and everything we fear, and letting go of this need for control and trusting in the process. Trusting in the process leads to new ideas, ideas we are free to pursue because we are not enslaved to the rigid thinking that is the result of fear.

Peace

We speak of *peace* as though it were a concept we really understand. We believe that peace means that at a given moment we are not engaged in the active killing of other human beings. But peace has little to do with war or its absence. Peace is not the opposite of war, but rather the opposite of fear.

Peace has no parameters, whereas fear is finite. Peace is limitless, and fear has walls and boundaries. This dichotomy helps explain why it is so difficult for most people to understand what it means to be at peace. It is extremely difficult to grasp the significance of being free. Most think freedom is just another version of the finite, but it is very much an entirely different concept.

The complete openness of mind and spirit that lives at peace with itself and others has no guidelines. We have very little experience or training in how to deal with something as vast and free as freedom. It is disconcerting and produces great anxiety when we have to deal with the infinite possibilities of the possible. All that we have seen, felt, been taught, experienced in our lives only reinforces the need to be bound.

The walls of fear keep us comfortable. They prevent uncertainty from entering. But at the same time they prevent options from being apparent and available. The walls of fear are secure, reinforcing what we have been told. They find ratification over and over again in the "real" world. The more we fear "enemies," the higher the walls grow, until finally they are so high that they block out any possibility of anything else entering. And then they become their own reality, and the possible is forever excluded.

The irony is that once our viewpoint changes and we begin to see what peace really means, the concept is something so simple, so apparent, that we cannot imagine how we could ever have missed it. That is why these Six Simple Principles are truly simple. As long as our lives have failed to cross over that subtle, unimaginably thin line, we truly are unable to understand what it all means. The only boundaries that exist at this new level are the limits we create for ourselves. The only rules are those we invent and agree to play by. Our personal history is unimportant, because at this place we can be anything we want to be and can disregard our own past, which has kept us bound for our entire lives. When we are short of the place of peace, we feel that we must continue to carry the chains that have bound us since our childhood, as though to let go of them would leave us without any sort of identity.

We need but to look out into the world to see the processes of restriction in practice. The real struggle is not what we read about in the newspaper or see on the evening news. It is not about this war or that, nor about this monetary problem or that. It is not about one nation invading another. It is not about environmental damage or economic conditions. Those are only the symptoms of the underlying, very deeply rooted issue: We are not at peace. And we are not at peace because we lack self-worth. The symptoms are what we talk about when we cannot or will not face the fact that we are afraid of change because we are not at peace. The symptoms are the burned toast of our collective lives.

Our battles are not about what they seem to be about, but rather are about the need some people have to coerce the natural process of change into the mold of restriction. We war against those seeking modifications, however small, in this continuation of repressive ideas. Revolutions of every sort are in reality the process of change struggling to manifest itself. We may consider revolutions to be good or bad, having good or bad motives, but all revolutions seek change and so will be met with resistance. The ideas about freedom for everyone, whether they be women seeking control over their lives, or the poor seeking a way out of the oppression of the rich, are only the forces of equilibrium in competition with the forces of restriction. These forces are the *yang* pulling the *yin*, and the *yin* bringing the *yang* into existence. Instead of seeing change as natural, we resist.

There are other examples of trying to restrict by force the natural process of change. These are attempts to restrict freedom of thought or action. They take the form of burning the book that says things we do not like. They are restrictions on thought in the name of banning pornography or passing obscenity laws. They are laws against flag burning. Restricting freedom of choice in reading, viewing, expressing, procreating and even dying are all about maintenance of the status quo.

Rather than allow for these sorts of freedom, which involve the process of change, those who are afraid want to keep the situation out of balance, out of equilibrium. They do so by force, either physical force or the force of repressive laws and economic policies. Of course, to the afraid it appears just the opposite, since they see the world as being out of balance. It is they who are trying to restore harmony; that is their view of the truth.

That there is a direct and traceable relationship among personal peace, personal freedom, and world peace is beyond question. What we see as external events, seemingly remote and unconnected from us, are in fact nothing but reflections of our own personal fears, anxieties, and paranoias. To change the way we look at the world and see ourselves as integral parts of the universe is a fundamentally different point of view. Trying to change the outer world before we change our inner one will lead only to failure. When each of us is no longer at war internally, we will resist being pushed into war with others. When each of us accepts responsibility for cleaning up our own small worlds, the larger world may become safe to live in. And when we all change our personal viewpoints about money, we may be able to begin the process of changing our external world as it concerns money. A change in "reality" can follow only when our personal morality changes.

Some Taoist Specifics

How do we translate this spirituality into practical politics? Politics today is nothing but war by other means. Little by way of fresh ideas comes from our elected leaders, except to war or to bluster as though we were going to war. By war, I mean not only killing war but monetary war, creating enmity among ourselves by having to share meager financial resources. Seeing one group yelling at another about salaries or Medicare or such is reminiscent of war, if only a bit less bloody.

The new world order, which is clearly not very much in place at this time, seems but a rehash of the old order with different actors. Governmental economic policies are as outdated as governmental war policies. The huge gap between what small segments of our society have as compared with other, larger segments is evidence that these policies are not working. Our long-range views have not matured. Though years ago it was written that the age of the nation state has passed, little has changed in the reality of the way we look at the world, since the nation state seems to remain primary. Lines on the map remain artificial and examples of coercion, of not letting the Earth be a single unit.

One concrete way we can begin to change these real-world issues is by examining how we participate, or indeed fail to participate, in the political process. The age of the nation state may in theory have passed, but that form of government continues to be the representative way of relating to one another on the planet, at this time and for the foreseeable future. Given the rise of extranational corporations, the transmigration of people, pollution, and economics, whether the nation-state view remains pertinent in the future is an open question. Now the "country" is the primary entity for global relationships, and so we must continue to work within that concept. Taoism is about going with the natural forces, and for this purpose, the natural forces are still the political process.

Surely it must be painfully obvious that, although Gulf War I occurred during a Republican administration and with a Democratic Congress, other wars in our history have been led by Democratic administrations and Republican Congresses and by other such combinations of political parties, some now defunct. And even though there may have been an opposition party in Congress, its opposition was nominal at best, because those whom we elected represented our own war mentality. So there was an empty debate about the war question, a debate about fringe issues, about "how" and "when" and not about "whether."

It therefore seems appropriate to look at the role that political parties outside the mainstream may play in the process of changing the way we look at the world. The time has come when old fashioned political thinking must give way to new ideas that can only come from new forms of political organization. The two major parties, which are really one, are so vested in the status quo—both in terms of the way we elect people to office and the way we think about the world—that to expect real change from them is all but impossible. These parties, which grew out of a different era, seem unable because of their vested interests to offer anything resembling new ideas to deal with the complexity of problems faced by the world today.

Indeed, the United States today is so diversified in what its people want that the two parties cannot possibly offer anything but homogenized pap, the better to appeal to everyone. We have today what Alvin Toffler called a "mosaic democracy,"[6] which makes having but two parties no longer relevant or useful.

It may be time to look toward a parliamentary system of government, in which small voices have greater power, or at least power commensurate with their population. Such a system, which of course would require a constitutional amendment to achieve, would give each of the minority positions an opportunity to have an impact on the process and would run less risk of alienating those who feel the political system is out of touch with their ideas, which results in the default of the vote that so characterizes today's apathy. We have come to accept, as another buzzword, that "majority rules" is somehow carved into stone and immutable. Who made that up? It is a non-Taoist concept, for it limits us to either/or instead of allowing multiplicity of choice, which we find uncomfortable. Many democratic nations, such as Canada, England, and Germany, have parliamentary systems that seem to work well. Taoist ideas hold that having many choices, rather than trying to restrict every concept into only two parties, allows for more natural political ideas to flourish.

Alternatively, even within the two-party system, we might think about voting for a third party. Some may believe that a vote for an alternative candidate is a wasted vote. What is a vote, anyway? It is one way, not the only way, but one way we can each of us make our own personal statement. If that vote is to represent our personal view, then we must forget the seeming impracticality of the vote and say, with all of our heart, "This is what I believe in." Our vote must reflect our deepest concerns, our deepest beliefs, and our deepest conscience. To vote for a candidate because he or she (mostly he, I'm afraid) has a better chance of winning or seems the lesser of two evils, when that candidate represents little, if anything, for which we stand, is truly offensive to that deepest conscience. As long as we tell future candidates that we are willing to accept mediocrity, hypocrisy, and outright deceit, the more we cast our precious voice for them simply because they are running on a major ticket, the more we defer our integrity and our morality, the less chance we have to ever effectuate change through the political process.

It is well to remember that today's major political parties were not always major parties. For example, the Republican Party was once merely the Republican party, and started in the 1850s as an antislavery party. It is irrational to say that just because starting a new party will take a long time to show results, we should therefore continue to vote for parties that do not reflect our view.

And what has this myth, this notion of not "wasting" our votes, given us over the recent past? What has this idea produced by way of fundamental change? Has it eliminated war? Has it improved our economics and made life better for the underprivileged? Has it lessened the pollution of our air, water, and ecosystems? Has it created a vibrant and growing job base? Has it created a moral society? Indeed, in terms of even 50 years, a mere millisecond in the history of time, what real changes have been wrought because we were willing to sacrifice our personal beliefs to vote for candidate A, who did not represent who we were or what we felt but who had a better chance of winning? We have to confront the myth that we are "wasting" our votes and open our minds to new ideas.

Until we are willing to advance the cause of people who actually stand for the issues that we believe are necessary in the search for peace, we shall be forever relegated to justifying the deed of our compromise in the name of some illusory and, in truth, false benefit. It seems that we have forgotten, in the cause of pragmatism, that we have an obligation to ourselves to make morality part of the decision-making process.

It is well to remember the discussion earlier about work. Similar thoughts as those about voting must go through our minds when we decide just how much we are willing to lose of ourselves to earn a living. Again, money and the outer world are closely connected. If indeed we do not respect ourselves enough to be truthful to our own integrity, then how can we, in all honesty, expect respect from those who would lead us? If we do not love ourselves enough to be faithful to our beliefs, how can we expect love from others? By going along with leaders who promise one thing in order to get elected, and as soon as the ballots are counted immediately do the exact opposite, we reflect our collective lack of self-worth. We fail to demand integrity from these leaders, even as we rue their lack of the same.

At the heart of any outer-world change is a personal inner change that each of us must go through. We must recognize our own lack of wholeness, our own lack of internal soundness, our own lack of freedom, before we can translate it into objective conduct. Taoist principles mean being free enough to open ourselves to new ideas, knowing that they can only lead to change, which is the natural way. So there is yet another option for changing the direction in which we are headed: If we ourselves are aware of alternative ways of seeing the world, then we will look for candidates who embody the spirit of the Tao— even though it would be a great surprise indeed to have anyone actively campaign on such a premise. Once we recognize how we, in our individual lives, refuse to deal with problems, refuse to face reality, refuse to talk about solutions and choose instead to blame the other, we may recognize the leaders who espouse Taoist ideas.

Taoist thinking is about cooperation, not confrontation. It is about following the natural course of events instead of trying to coerce them, control them, force them into other outcomes. But seeing the long-term implications of our actions, instead of deciding things simply on the basis of immediate need, is an alien idea to most of us.

Other Choices for Our Money

War is our most significant expenditure based on short-term thinking. With a change in our approach to the world, to ourselves, we can eliminate this waste and turn our resources toward solving some of the problems we face. All the trillions of dollars spent on war, on building nuclear missiles, submarines, not-quite radar-evading airplanes, and the like, certainly did nothing to prevent the terrorist-style attack in 1993 on the World Trade Center in New York or the slaughter in Bosnia. If we are going to prevent those types of wars, then we must seek out real solutions—and these solutions have nothing to do with armaments. They have to do with understanding others.

With the budgetary savings we would realize by not pursuing war as a means to an end, we could begin the process of spending our money toward the common good. A portion of that money could go to the states and cities who are on the front line of our social problems, enabling them to reopen closed hospitals, provide economic assistance in racially troubled and economically depressed areas, helping to reduce the problems that are so intrinsically tied to lack of opportunity.

These monies could be used to fund hospital and medical care for the poor, and to increase aid to schools so that education would again take priority and students would not have their dreams cut short. This might in turn reap benefits such as decreasing the social drain of teenage pregnancies, school dropouts, and the like and making us more competitive in the world economy. We could fund child care and public health programs. A portion of these savings could go toward a comprehensive health care system so that tens of millions of us do not live in fear of bankruptcy should we become ill.

A large sum of savings could go toward environmental cleanup, so that we could stop killing ourselves from the inside.

What would you do if you had $300 billion a year to spend in making the world a better place?

These suggestions are certainly not intended to be exhaustive of new ideas we can approach with new financial resources. As I have said, the Tao is not a blueprint. The exact process we choose must be developed by us, by political leaders chosen by us with our new ideas, free of the constraints of old ideas. Each of these new proposals will be, to be certain, met with laughs, and sneers, and who knows what else. We all giggle nervously at the truth. But Taoist teachings show us that the way in which we have looked at the world so far has resulted in war and death, and that unless we begin to let go of the need to control others and allow them to be free, we will surely continue this process of dying.

With enough self-assurance to allow others the freedom we ourselves want, we may have no need for weapons. We may have no need for repression. We may have no need for war. Most importantly, our ability to accept seemingly "radical" proposals depends entirely on our ability to let go of our need for control over the world and for certainty.

Continuing to see the world in the old way means that we will continue to spend our money in the old way. Continuing to see the world in the old way means that we will continue to see ourselves as divided from our problems. Continuing to see the world in the old

way means that we will never be able to accept solutions that say We, not just They, must change.

These ideas are radical only because they require
us to let go of our seemingly innate way of viewing the
planet and its problems. But when we can look at
these ideas without our preconceived "they'll never
work" attitude, if we can examine them free of our fear
of anything new, we might see that they are only
common sense.

A Personal Note

When it comes to the broadest concept about money, we are living in denial. We are pretending we are okay when we are not, partly out of fear of coping with the consequences of knowing the truth. We know something is deeply wrong with our entire economic and social structure, but we fear changing anything too dramatically. We look under the lamppost, precisely *because* we know we will not find anything there.

Fear becomes the rationale, if not always expressed or understood, underlying our lack of concern for others. Fear is behind our apathy for the fate of the entirety of humanity. We fear exposing the fallacies that we have lived with for eons. We seem only to have the need to get for ourselves, because to do otherwise somehow creates insecurity. I suspect these feelings are not well defined in those who exhibit them. Truly, those involved do not see themselves acting out of fear; rather, they call it protection of their legitimate rights, which they perceive as being somehow vested. Surely they are vested, if at all, only in Man's world, for they are certainly not in Nature's.

Freedom is really the ability to let go of that which appears to be vested. We are not being truthful to ourselves, to our sensitivities, or to our fears, and so our dreams and ideals are set accordingly low—for if all we care about is our immediate welfare, whether individual, business, or national, then our vision is bound to come up short. Failing to be truthful on an individual level leads inevitably to a lowering of standards for the society as a whole, as we carry our diminished ideals into the "real world."

> Without soulful fathers, our society is left with mere reason and ideology as guides. Then we suffer collective fatherlessness: not having a clear national direction; giving the spoils of a wealthy economy to a few; finding only rare examples of deep morality, law, and community; not seeking out odyssey because we prefer the solid ground of opinion and ideology. To set out on the sea is to risk security, yet that risky path may be the only way to the father.[1]

The path to change is very long. But that does not diminish the value of seeking to attain our objective. None of us is at the ideal place yet, for if we were, none of this quest would be necessary. If you follow the Tao in your personal life, you may be admired for having a peaceful viewpoint. If you follow the Tao in your objective life, attempting to apply these same principles in politics or in solving the social and economic problems we face, you may be scorned, called a purist, and an idealist. You should be pleased by this attempt at derision, for it has always been the visionary, the dreamer, the idealist who has created change.

I have this vision, a vision which has developed over the years, of what I want life to be, and the struggle in which I am engaged is in trying to make that vision a reality. It brings a fair amount of frustration, as you can imagine. In my own evolution, I am burdened with the need for achieving that which I have set out to achieve, and nothing short of that achievement will allow me peace. Getting there, with all of its ups and downs and backsliding, is not only part of the process, it *is* the process. Striving to achieve harmony and balance with the universe, with God, is what Taoism is about.

And this need for purity spills over into my world view, because the great issues facing us might be so simply resolved and yet the solutions are more illusive than they appear. To compromise is the norm, and yet it does not appear that compromise has brought anything but evil, danger, and unhappiness for large numbers of us. Indeed, the lack of desire for purity and perfection has seemingly increased with the passage of time. As more of us are willing to let the large things slide, the more they do, and as a result the issues seem larger and less solvable, leading in turn to a greater willingness to compromise yet again.

As I have mentioned, we rarely question immoral acts when we band together and commit them collectively, in the name of our "nation," but we would never do these acts individually. Political scientists and theoreticians tell us that we cannot impose the ethics of individuals on the conduct of governments because they are too complex and varied. And yet there are fundamental truths, truths that go to the heart of all morality, which should apply to governments, to businesses, to collective action. And yet we fail to insist on at least striving to reach such standards.

When I speak of peace, of a vision that I have, I am told that I am idealistic, unrealistic, that these things can never come to pass. I find it difficult to understand how we have arrived at this condition in which what passes for realism is the acquiescence of each of us to the torture, murder, and repression of many millions of people around the world. Since when did the quiet concession to the pollution of our air and water become realistic? Is it realistic to allow unemployment, homelessness, ignorance, and hunger in the midst of plenty? If realism means what is must always be, then these tortured definitions of reality are, I suspect, examples of realism. When I suggest, however, that the status quo need not remain so forever, that there are concrete and yes, realistic, things we can each of us do to effectuate change in the process, I am met with resistance. When I say that what is realistic is *not* fateful and absolute adherence to the current state of affairs, but rather a recognition of the problems we face and a willingness to accept the challenge of change, I am scoffed at in some circles. What passes for realism in the majority of cases seems to be fatalistic coping, and the implication that our futures are merely a slavish copy of our past.

When people are unwilling to dream, then ideals must, by definition, be lowered. Those who run for office, from the highest office to the lowest, rise only to the level of competency demanded of them by those casting the vote. Perhaps, someday, the successful candidate will have to meet these qualifications:

> WANTED: One (1) visionary, able to see long-term implications of action, unafraid to acknowledge the male, female nature of humanity, positive self-image, daring, intuitive without disdaining the rational, spiritual, M/F, EOE. Philosophers, writers, artists given preference. Good salary and benefits. Opportunity for travel.

I know that I am a purist. I know that my vision is not shared by others. I know, however, that I am either blessed or cursed with the need to pursue my vision despite all of its frustrations. And yet, because I am a pragmatic purist, I am also aware that the pearl in the oyster is only created by the intrusion of sand.

Epilogue

The Tao of Money is clearly about more than money. But, like the *Tao Te Ching*, which describes a universe in which everything is connected to everything else, *The Tao of Money* says money must be seen as a part of all other social issues. Money is not only a root cause of those social issues but a product of them as well.

Everything is about money when we define money in its broadest sense to include security, peace, war, repression, and freedom. And when we so define money, we cannot but see that our handling of money and its related issues in our personal lives determines to a large degree how money and money-related issues are handled in the outer world.

And so the Six Simple Principles for Achieving Financial Harmony tells us that our personal financial harmony is no different from and indeed can be the basis for worldwide financial harmony. The ways we look at money personally, our ability to reach a place of harmony personally, have a direct impact on our ability to translate that harmony into the larger money issues.

There is no way we can separate money from these same "larger" issues; recognizing this, it is futile to attempt to change these outer issues without first or concurrently changing our own views about money. Changing how we see money requires us to examine the very essence of who we are and how we feel about ourselves.

I realize that there will be many who say that my views are too long-term and that we need answers now. I agree that we need answers now, but the answers we need now must be answers that solve our problems instead of exacerbate them.

Fundamental change is the most difficult challenge any of us face in our lives, but that difficulty does not mean we should pretend such fundamental change is not one way to peace. Instead of looking under the lamppost, it is time to look for our keys where we dropped them.

> The brain is wider than the sky,
>   For, put them side by side,
> The one the other will include
>   With ease, and you beside.

The brain is deeper than the sea,
    For, hold them, blue to blue,
The one the other will absorb,
    As sponges, buckets do.

The brain is just the weight of God,
    For, lift them, pound for pound,
And they will differ, if they do,
    As syllable from sound.[1]

Notes

Notes to The Premise

1. A version of some of these ideas previously appeared in *Whole Life Times* 117, January 1992, p. 9.

2. HENRY DAVID THOREAU, *Walden*, (1854), (New York: Holt, Rinehart and Winston, Inc., 1961), p. 5.

3. IVAN HOFFMAN, *The Tao of Love* (Rocklin, California: Prima Publishing, 1993), p. 5. © 1993 by Ivan Hoffman.

4. ALVIN TOFFLER, *PowerShift: Knowledge, Wealth, and Violence at the Edge of the 21st Century* (New York: Bantam Books, 1991), p. 79. Copyright © 1990 by Alvin Toffler and Heidi Toffler. Used by permission of the publisher.

Notes to Principle 1

1. WILLIAM BLAKE, *A Divine Image* (ca. 1794), *English Poetry and Prose of the Romantic Movement*, ed. George Benjamin Woods (Chicago: Scott, Foresman and Company, 1950 edition), p. 186.

2.   WILLIAM WORDSWORTH, *The World Is Too Much With Us; Late and Soon* [1806, 1807]: *English Poetry and Prose of the Romantic Movement,* ed. George Benjamin Woods (Chicago: Scott, Foresman and Company, 1950 edition), p. 328.

3.   MARSHA SINETAR, *Do What You Love, The Money Will Follow: Discovering Your Right Livelihood* (New York: Dell Publishing, 1989), p. 198. Copyright © 1987 by Dr. Marsha Sinetar. Used by permission of the publisher.

Notes to Principle 2

1.   HOFFMAN, *The Tao of Love,* p. 36.

2.   ALAN WATTS, *Tao: The Watercourse Way* (New York: Pantheon Books, 1975), p. 43. Copyright © 1975 by Mary Jane Yates Watts, Literary Executrix of the Will of Alan W. Watts, deceased. Used by permission of the publisher.

3.   THOMAS CLEARY, trans. and ed. *The Tao of Politics: Lessons of the Masters of Huainan* (Boston & London: Shambhala, 1990), p. viii. © 1990 by Thomas Cleary. Reprinted by arrangement with Shambhala Publications, Inc., 300 Massachusetts Ave., Boston, MA 02115.

Notes to Principle 3

1.   MILDRED NEWMAN & BERNARD BERKOWITZ with JEAN OWEN, *How to Be Your Own Best Friend* (New York: Random House, 1971), p. 33. Copyright © 1971 by Mildred Newman and Bernard Berkowitz. Used by permission of the publisher.

2.   ARCHIE J. BAHM, *Tao Teh King by Lao Tzu Interpreted as Nature and Intelligence* (Translation of Tao 22), (New York: Continuum, 1990), p. 27. Copyright © 1958, 1986 by Frederick Ungar Publishing Co. Used by permission of the author.

3.   O. HENRY, *A Cosmopolite in a Café* (*The Complete Works of O. Henry*) (New York: Doubleday & Company, Inc., 1953), Vol. 1, p. 13.

Notes to Principle 5

1.   For numerous similar, if less "radical," examples of reform in government, see DAVID OSBORNE and TED GAEBLER, *Reinventing Government: How the Entrepreneurial Spirit Is Transforming the Public Sector* (New York: Plume Books, 1993). Copyright © David Osborne and Ted Gaebler, 1992.

2.   A version of these ideas appeared in *Whole Life Times* 119, March 1992, p. 9.

3.   WATTS, *Tao: The Watercourse Way,* p. 82.

Notes to Principle 6

1.   ROBERT B. REICH, *The Work of Nations: Preparing Ourselves for 21st Century Capitalism* (referring to the writings of J. A. Hobson), (New York: Vintage Books, 1992), p. 31. Copyright © 1991, 1992 by Robert B. Reich. Used by permission of the publisher.

2.   BAHM, *Tao Teh King by Lao Tzu Interpreted as Nature and Intelligence* (Translation of Tao 74), p. 64.

3.   A version of these ideas appeared in *Whole Life Times* 117, January 1992, p. 9.

4.   WATTS, *Tao: The Watercourse Way*, p. 82.

5.   HOFFMAN, *The Tao of Love*, p. 14.

6.   TOFFLER, *Powershift: Knowledge, Wealth, and Violence at the Edge of the 21st Century*, p. 245.

Note to A Personal Note

1.   THOMAS MOORE, *Care of the Soul: A Guide for Cultivating Depth and Sacredness in Everyday Life* (New York: HarperCollins Publishers, Inc., 1992), pp. 38-39. Copyright © 1992 by Thomas Moore. Used by permission of the publisher.

Note to Epilogue

1.   EMILY DICKINSON, *Selected Poems & Letters of Emily Dickinson*, ed. Robert N. Linscott (New York: Doubleday Anchor, 1959), p. 98. Used by permission of Wendy T. Linscott as Executrix of the Estate of Robert N. Linscott.

INDEX

Also by Ivan Hoffman . . .

In seeking to know the nature of love—the way to love and to be loved—we can learn much by seeking out the wisdom of ancient thinking, the wisdom of Taoism. Ivan Hoffman has incorporated the spirituality of Taoism, which dates back 2,500 years, with his personal and psychological reflections to make this ancient wisdom relevant today.

To love, we must first learn about ourselves. We must gain freedom from the need to control or to blame—others or ourselves—and to learn that we are one with the universe; in this oneness there is comfort and serenity. Only when we can let go of ourselves can we be open to be loved by others.

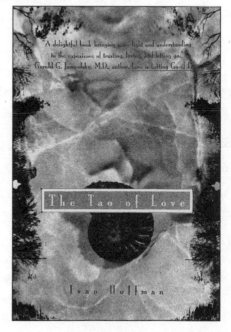

A delightful book bringing more light and understanding to the experience of trusting, loving, and letting go.
—Gerald G. Jampolsky, M.D., author, *Love is Letting Go of Fear*

FILL IN AND MAIL . . . TODAY

PRIMA PUBLISHING
P.O. BOX 1260BK
ROCKLIN, CA 95677

USE YOUR VISA/MC AND ORDER BY PHONE
(916) 786-0426 (M–F 9:00 A.M.–4:00 P.M. PST)

Please send me the following title:

Quantity	Title	Amount
_____	*The Tao of Love* $9.95	_____

Subtotal	$ _____
Postage & Handling $3.95 per book	$ _____
7.25 % Sales Tax (California only)	$ _____
TOTAL (U.S. funds only)	$ _____

☐ Check enclosed for $_____ (payable to Prima Publishing)

Charge my   ☐ MasterCard   ☐ Visa

Account No. _____   Exp. Date_____

Signature _____

Your Printed Name _____

Address _____

City/State/Zip _____

Daytime Telephone _____

Satisfaction is guaranteed— or your money back!
Please allow three to four weeks for delivery.
THANK YOU FOR YOUR ORDER